New Birth

New Birth

Faith, Culture, and Church as Family

Pius Ojara, SJ

WIPF & STOCK · Eugene, Oregon

NEW BIRTH
Faith, Culture, and Church as Family

Wipf & Stock
An imprint of Wipf and Stock Publishers
199 W. 8th Ave., Suite 3
Eugene, OR 97401

www.wipfandstock.com

ISBN 13: 978-1-4982-5362-8

Manufactured in the U.S.A.

I dedicate this work to
Ms. Catherine Kelly
and
Fr. James Duffy, SJ,
two priceless friends.

Contents

Acknowledgments

THIS WORK WAS A labor of passion for the joy of living and for living in particular ways. I wrote this work in contexts where the wise and the foolish, fear and hope, and the ugly and beautiful mix and clasp hands in the very heart of life and living. Writing this book called forth the tragic sense of life as well as the lighthearted beauty of being alive. This work, in one sense, presents my growth and accompanying desire to illuminate and understand what happens in the day-to-day task of living the Christian faith in a cultural context as well as growing in wholesome relationships.

I wrote this work in three different places. I started to write this book when I was in Berkeley, California. I then continued with writing when I came to teach at Arrupe College, Harare, Zimbabwe. As I concluded the work, I was in Kampala, Uganda. So I would like to thank various people I met and lived with in the three different places because they offered me the space, experience, and tone for deepening my convictions and appreciation of the insights that this book contains. The variety of these experiences helped me see personally how God continues to work wonderfully in the lives of his people. He continues to renew his Church through the outpouring of his spirit of love in the lives and relationships of people. Above all, God truly and continually rewards human efforts.

Friends have been particularly helpful in shaping the way I thought about the different issues I deal with in the book. In my life's journey I have been blessed to have some very good people choose me as their friend. Because of this, my life has been graced by people whose relationships with me remain deeply personal and enlivening. I rejoice in these friendships that happened in my life and which I now cherish very much. In this regard I am grateful for my delightful and enduring friendship with the following: Ms. Catherine Kelly, Bobby Dyakema, Ms. Donna Smith, Mrs. Joy Kimemiah, Mrs. Marceline Cannon, Sr. Stellamarris Ihejeto, HHCJ, Fr. James Duffy, SJ, Fr. Timothy Mannat, SJ, Fr. Joseph Afulo, SJ, Mr. Shawn

Acknowledgments

Wehan, Fr. Isaac Kiyaka, SJ, Fr. John Paul, SJ, Fr. Uwem Akpan, SJ, and Fr. Anthony Wach, SJ.

Obviously, too, I draw a lot of wisdom from a number of people who I encountered in my school life in the recent past. On their shoulders I certainly stand. These include Profs. Donald Gelpi, SJ, Howlands T. Sanks, SJ, and Gina-Hens Piazza, all at the Jesuit School of Theology in Berkeley, California. The influence of their thoughts remains unmistakable in this work.

I must now note that I remain particularly grateful to many Jesuits of the Eastern Africa Province of the Society of Jesus, who have always been supportive and encouraging of my writing. The body of the Society of Jesus has always supported me and continues to make it possible for me to continue writing.

Indeed, I have come to increasingly believe that fun, drama, and beauty mark human life with their golden ripples, as it were. Obviously, insights from these perspectives on life have fashioned the content of this work. I believe that this work brings with it a large sense of life's journey together with its triumphs, startling reversals, and unexpected twists and turns.

Introduction

WE LIVE IN A world increasingly marked by impassioned selfish-ness that particularly manifests itself in consumerism and he-donism by means of which anything seems legitimate. And within this mounting culture of license, a primary question that appears to guide the activities of most people has become, "What is in it for me?" Often within such a question there exists little concern and care for others so that considerations about others at best take the self-interested form of "my people or my group." And yet a world permeated with such a sensibility offers little security for people and their relationships with one another. Scandals and obsession with scandals become the staples of the media and the excitement of the people. All tolerance of human frailty and ambiguity lose their practical sense and significance. In these circumstances the Church can also lose its focus in this world; she risks buying into the prevailing world sense, or in response to the state of affairs, she risks taking on backward thinking instead of appropriating forward thinking. Subsequently, when people cannot trust each other relationally, they live life with anxiety and paralyzing fears. It's no won-der, then, that marital breakdown, single parenting, children growing up without father figures, and the growing number of street people with teenage pregnancies continue to increase in our contemporary world. At the same time, it must be added, we have a few prophets in our world to whom the media does not seem to pay much attention.

Nevertheless, the enfleshment of God in our midst resolves, once and for all, the life-transforming questions of the inherent worth, dignity, and lovableness of all people. In the Spirit God dwells wonderfully in the hearts of all living people. God takes abode among people so that life, light, and love become constant features of people's lives. The incarnation (i.e., God becoming a human being) implies that the unfailingly honest and faithful God continually brings light and hope into a world of darkness, oppression, and despair. Through the incarnation Christians celebrate the triumph of a religious vision of justice and peace over militarism, social injustice, and oppression.

Through the incarnation, Christians observe and admit the dawn of a new spirit of generosity and light, of love of neighbor, and of loyalty to the living God who promises life based on justice and peace by infusing his spirit in the minds and hearts (i.e., consciousness) of men and women of good will. God accomplishes this task through the life and mission of individuals as well as liberation struggles involving entire people who seek to remake the world by working to transform the exploitative and oppressive political and social order. This fact also means that the beautiful message of Christian hope takes place in a world not yet fully redeemed. Thus, the incarnation basically incorporates a profound message of hope where Christians can look forward to a different world that they can help bring about through their efforts.

In effect, hope amidst social darkness and the ethos of selfishness and materialism remains intrinsic to God's purposes for human wellbeing. With hope people experience and express care and mutual support. That is also to say that powers of greed, selfishness, and domination do not have the final say on the reality of human existence. But the risk always remains that believers can distort true hope when they try to make their ideals consistent with human arrangements based on inequality and domination.

In light of the foregoing considerations, the invitation of Christian discipleship through the countervailing and transforming metaphor of the Church as family can provide a positive way that offers an enduring sense of security, unselfishness, and self-giving. The call of the gospel remains that of relational trust, commitment, and warmth. The gospel asks of Christians that they go out of and beyond themselves out of faith, love, and hope. This also means, for instance, that the exercise of authority can only remain in the serving of the community, which consists of bringing together the diverse members of the human community.

Jesus Christ establishes the Christian perspective toward life as a whole. He awakens Christian hope and renews and deepens the Christian way of seeing things so that humanity succeeds and triumphs. Christ assures Christians of the promises of life in spite of the fact that deep struggles mark our identities, values, and purpose. This assurance implies passionately engaging in the struggle for a fuller humanity. God choosing to become a human being means that humanity and God cannot be separated or brought apart. In effect, intrinsic value and dignity belong to the uniqueness and relational totality of every person from beginning to the end. Or again, God makes the human condition his very own. We cannot, then, deny God without in some way denying our humanity. To exile God from the world coincides, in a certain sense, with impoverishing and alienating ourselves from our own truth, which remains inseparable from love itself. Thus, in Christ we find the meaning of true humanity, of true freedom, and of being fully alive. Every human being has a reason for being as our life of the spirit grows.

Historically, then, the Church aligns herself with the mission of Jesus in history, the bringer of abundant life. The reason lies in the fact that the human experience of Jesus Christ always takes up and realizes the eternal value and significance necessary for appreciating and living the wonder of this life. Eternity lends urgency and beauty to the gift of this life; perennial value gives significance to our roles in life. Our unique and precious life needs a badge of eternity for its lasting validation and enduring purpose. Or again, our amazing sense of dignity and great sense of responsibility stems from the endowment of eternal value. The Church's confident alignment with the mission of Christ then inseparably involves the promotion of truth, justice, harmony, and unity in a world beset by prejudice, discrimination, oppression, and all kinds of enslavements and dividedness. In other words, the Church constantly seeks to respectfully walk the path of charity and uprightness, which enables people to adjust their desires to the needs and demands of others. Such a path also remains laced with the spirit of true generosity that stimulates and actuates liberative freedom.

Of course, we must not forget that the originating living figure of Christ that we frequently appropriate comes from the New Testament, where we find him presented in multiple appearances and postures of availability. And when the excellence of the humanity and person of Jesus grasps us, we experience a union of commitment and values with him. Then the refreshing and liberating character of our interactive and interpretative encounter with the living figure of Jesus marks our own patterns of Christian living. In concrete living, however, the experience or the image of Jesus that we receive and appropriate commonly comes from the varied words, witness, and behaviors of the community of Christian believers.

At the same time, we cannot, as a community of disciples of Jesus, separate the path of charity and uprightness from the path of justice. Without a doubt, we act justly when we honor and work for the respect, wellbeing, and rights of our neighbors, whoever they may be. This fact also means taking into account and appreciating the judgments and freedom of others. In this sense, Christian charity, uprightness, and justice relate very closely. As Christians, however, we do justice when we also link it with the warmth and understanding of the gospel and the personal following of Christ. In this way, charity, uprightness, and justice remain truly themselves through concrete commitments and concrete issues that enable people to live in dignity and freedom in their lives. In other words, charity, uprightness, and justice make relationships and communities humane, concrete, and realistic.

Noticeably, too, when people do love one another, they can be together and encourage one another. And as they support each other, they strengthen one another. Conversely, the failure to love commonly leads to all kinds of discrimination, violence, and injustices. Furthermore, when we protect love from aberration, we protect the best in ourselves and build up a future of humanity. In light of this understanding, the Church sees and identifies herself as an efficacious agent of love. This very fact also straightforwardly turns the Church into a vehicle of hope. It simply cannot be overlooked, then, that in order to brim with hope[1] as is proper for her life, the community called the Church needs to continually stand against domination, individualism, and communalism or collectivism. In her true identity, the Church always stands in opposition to brutish excitements, spiteful vengeance, vile abuses, and acting according to whims and caprices. The fundamental message of the Church lays emphasis on

---

1. Hope means that we approach life with cautious optimism, confidence, and conviction that the normalcy and prosperity we labor for truly beckon us. In view of this understanding, hope also holds that unarmed truth and unconditional availability, and not triumphant evil, bear the final word within human reality. Hope means, then, that victory and momentum for the fuller life can always come out of disorder, chaos, and frustrations. In addition, without hope, all sense of justice and truth lose their concrete and authentic significance. Accordingly, when hope motivates us, we can resourcefully persevere through the difficulties and challenges of life. Against this background, Christian hope anchors itself in the deep religious sense that God continually cares for his own people in history. Besides, Christian hope nourishes itself with the memory of real, beautiful experiences in history that sustained people through long, difficult times.

hope, equality in dignity, respect for persons, truthfulness, liberty, justice, and basic human rights for all.

The Church assumes the imperative and the struggle for the common welfare of men and women in different contexts and time. When the Church lives in her true identity, she incarnates discernment, tolerance, and fairness in human relations and arrangements in the world. This stance of the Church becomes particularly urgent as the processes of urbanization and globalization create highly mobile, basically anonymous, and precarious relationships among people. With the resulting anonymity and precariousness of life often comes the crumble of individual significance as well. In this context, the community called Church becomes prophetic when it refers constantly to vital individual human beings as irreplaceable for the Church's continuity in this world. Subsequently, in the Church we have the imperative to hold each person tenderly, trustingly, and deeply. When the community called Church marks itself with depth of human connections and the hope and joy of living, it illuminates and expands life in ways that enhance communication, collaboration, and communion among people. In this way, the church also expands the availability of people to live as best as they humanly can, which also implies both material development and spiritual growth.

The Church relevantly opposes, adopts, adapts, challenges, and transforms some cultural tendencies in which she incarnates herself. In so doing, elements of her life become adopted, adapted, assimilated, challenged, and transformed or even ignored. When we speak this way we refer to the liberating spirit that imbues the Church with its abiding sense of mission and identity in our deeply ambivalent world. Undoubtedly, then, respect for particular cultures allows different Christian communities (as incarnations of the Church) to have moral space, sensibility, and expressions of their own. It also means that different communities in the Church can enter into peaceful and mutual relations with one another within a context of human solidarity. In fact, when extraordinary inspiration springs from a concern with ordinary men and women, Christians proclaim the good news that finds flesh in the increasing acknowledgment of dialogue, justice, and peace as central to the character of Christian discipleship. In this way, the gospel encourages and strengthens the experience and expression of solidarity among people.

In point of fact, solidarity refers to human beings giving support through their sheer presence and concern for one another. It has its basis in the image of God or the divine filiation of every person, which finds concrete expression in living ties that originally link all people together. These living ties make people reach out to one another despite differences of race, creed, and culture. And the deep need for human beings to be together and appreciate each other's presence constitutes all basis of hope. That is also to say that generosity and reconciliation among people implies hope. In this regard, hope encourages good neighborliness, which makes it possible for people to meet each other as brothers and sisters of the same quality. In fact, we live hope in each of us as we positively influence decisions that affect our lives as human beings created in the image and likeness of God.

In other words, when the sense and experience of familyhood mark the community called the Church, they expand our capacity for care and responsibility for one another within a framework of shared humanity and the language of the intrinsic dignity of each person. This experience offers people the possibility and opportunities of trusting, hoping, and belonging through a widespread renewal of human relationships. People then lighten and brighten each other's lives with the spirit of compassion and love. The Church, then, creates a new vision of tomorrow from the triumphs of yesterday when she calls people to transcendence and new birth.

When people open themselves to the wisdom and care of one another, life together becomes commonplace. Additionally, people gain and expand the sense of who they can authentically become. As people count on one another, their trust and confidence in life also expand, not just in the arena of friendships and families, but also in the network of allies, associations, loyalties, and broad collaborations. In this way, however, being the Church does not equate with mere political connection or the issues of social attachments among people. The spiritual mandate of being the Church reveals an outpouring of God's outreach and friendship with people of all places, races, circumstances, and time. As a locus for growth of human relationships and communities, the Church plays an important role in offering pathways to the high point of integral friendships and positive relations among people. When this awareness imbues the lives of individual Christians, the Church truly fulfills her prophetic mission in this world.

In addition, the Church as a community of continual conversations heals life's wounds. As a community of trust and reverence that sanctions free exchanges among its members and between its members and the world, the Church brings with it a notion of being more than a social organism. As a vehicle of spiritual communion, then, the Church facilitates the fusion and bonding of relationships. The key challenge that faces the Church always has to do with the quality of human connections. This quality in human relationships goes beyond casual contacts and idle conversations. It implies life-giving warmth, reverence, service, good neighborliness, and above all, communities of familial care and friendships. Accordingly, vindictiveness, ugly pettiness, and disregard for the humanity of others contrast sharply with the spirit of being the Church.

For continuing relevance in the world, the Church needs conversion experiences. As the lifeline of faith, conversion enables the community called the Church to create personal space and autonomy (i.e., a totality of freedom and control) for its members. Conversion brings about reform in thinking and attitudes as well as ways of acting and imagining life. When a Christian converts, Jesus becomes the criterion who calls all to the true human likeness given to men and women by God. Pointedly, Christians realize that they make their life a gift of true and beautiful love if they follow in Jesus's footsteps. Here it becomes important to recognize that conversion re-awakens the vigor and vitality of human existence according to the light of Christ. The unity[2] that conversion sets off and actualizes forms the framework that enables us to initiate, cultivate, and sustain liberative activities, cooperative efforts, and cherished relationships. We then renew and improve the quality of individual and common life. Through conversion we open our hearts[3] in ways that make manifest divine presence and activity in actual decisions and conduct in this life. But this transformation happens if our judgments and choices (mentality) harmonize with the spirit of the gospel. In the end, conversion means, in part, that we repent of our sins and take care of injustices that blot the beauty of relational life.

When faith and conversion bind people together with a common sense of purpose, they foster deep feelings among the members of the community called Church. A deep feeling enlivens human relationships,

---

2. Unity here means functioning and living interactively as a result of friendships, partnership, and cooperation. To unite does not necessarily mean working in the same way. In this regard, it always helps if we do not confuse unity with conformity.

3. The heart symbolizes the deep spring of human activity and creativity that expresses our real selves.

enables loving presence, and breeds selflessness by means of which people pour out their lives in order to promote, serve, and care for the well-being of others. In holding, sustaining, and promoting a sense of togetherness among people this way, the Church furthers the cause of listening, affirmations, and respect among people. People can always transcend themselves at any given moment. When obligated to the good of one another, members of the Church strive for the fullness of the common good. Consciousness of others together with their needs makes the world a compassionate place in which authenticity and sharing can flourish.

Still, in our problematic world, a person can catch glimpses of a social and relational space already reconciled in and through fraternity. This fact means that people can celebrate life and engage the world positively. This fact also suggests that amidst much adversity the community called the Church can offer people much hope, encouragement, and a sustaining sense of significance. Seeing goodness in people, in spite of their conditions of living, belongs to the immediate gaze of the Church. The Church's way to spiritual fecundity enables people to re-create themselves anew constantly. This vision, which springs from the light of the Risen Christ, truly allows others to be others and perhaps become something more. When the Church lives her life as a pledge and responsibility, she nourishes dreams and prods the potential of individuals and of all living relationships among people. The value, weight, and harmony that living in the Spirit of Christ begets build up and provide a consciousness of social belonging. This consciousness, too, holds assurances and wellsprings of significance and growth in courage, endurance, vibrancy, and goodness.

Unreservedly, the nurturance that properly belongs to the Church remains one of enabling and promoting. This explains why the metaphor of the Church as a family[4] (inseparable from its countervailing notion and transformational character), the significance of healthy relationships, and inculturation[5] become pivotal tools that indicate the paths along which the Church can regularly walk prophetically. This

---

4. The metaphor of Church not only enables and empowers; it also plays functional and critical roles in the life of the community of disciples called the Church.

5. Inculturation refers to the working out of our understanding of faith and religious practices in conversation and prayer with local cultures, viz., African cultures in our present case. At any rate, the sparkle of inculturation stimulates, nourishes, and colors the cultural lives of believers with the values of the gospel. An inculturated faith constantly places the basic lives of its adherents in the presence of God.

also means, however, that the Church truly sympathizes with successes of life in our global world.

Without a doubt, when culture and faith mix in the Church as a family in creative ways, faith adds something new to culture and culture adds new elements to faith. A striving for newness takes place. Initially, culture and faith may seek domination or submission of the patterns and order of each other instead of the harmonious interrelation of a creative sort. Faith adds new principles of intentionality and awareness that continually relate to a given culture. And within the continual impulse of an inculturated faith, conflicts and strivings produce their own species of tensions through emergent qualities and development of an inner nisus of culture and faith. Inculturation thus produces creative diversification of faith and culture through their plural and spontaneous urges and tendencies, and a certain set of values becomes actualized. Then the continuities of faith and culture continually direct and modify each other in the realization of a higher and a more authentic unity.

When people tune in to one another in harmony in the Church as a family, the nexus of hope, the joy of living, and the iridescence of spirit come to fit together on the table fellowship of human coexistence. Invigorating the human community and human individuals with the spirit of fraternity, kinship, and liberative togetherness belongs to the Church's fundamental identity and mission. As a dwelling place of faith and love, the Church exists to bond, tend, befriend, embrace, and father all people together. The resulting care and listening frame build up a new kind of participation and an inclusive life that further recreates Church. A penchant for openness, acceptance, and positive definition of the self and of others enkindles and honors the symbol of the Church as family.

This book begins in chapter 1 with a consideration of faith and culture. This chapter identifies the family and the metaphor of the Church as family as foci of intimate linkage between faith and culture. The chapter addresses the foundational issue of coupling together faith and culture in order for the proclamation of the gospel to have its root in the very fabric of ordinary life. In a sense, the chapter presents a broad framework of understanding and for bringing together faith and culture. Chapter 2 deals with the case of active and continuous faith that engages reflection and the praxis of hope. The treatment of the vitality of active faith in this chapter engages a biblical text from the prophet Isaiah (Isa 40:1–11). When not merely sentimental or rhetorical, active faith affects the lived realities of people's contexts in ways that restore people to dignity even amidst the ravages and battering of experience.

While cognizant of the inescapable tensions, pains, and disappointment that lived experience brings, chapter 3 considers some key elements necessary for a satisfactorily functioning community called the Church. This chapter, in effect, urges wider forms of openness and great depth within the Church. Chapter 4 concerns itself with conversion as a pivot and organizing principle of the Church as family. In fact, conversion constitutes the prophetic heartbeat of the Church as family. Without the ongoing dynamism of conversion, the community called the Church easily comes to lack a deep spiritual base and *telos* or sense of purpose. The inner structure and resources of the Christian faith and lived experiences help enhance the appreciation of the need for conversion in the Church.

Chapter 5 discusses a few scriptural texts in order to bring to light or lift up some important elements and dynamics that build up the various perspectives and expressions of familyhood within the Church. And in chapter 6, some far-reaching considerations of emotional life and expectations as issues that affect the depth and quality of human relations take place. The focus remains on how to productively negotiate relational conflicts so that we increasingly make healthy relationships in concrete ways.

Understandably, the thrust of this work poses inevitable challenges to the living out of Christian discipleship. It also offers some opportunities to the community of Christian disciples. In the end, the impulses of this work accord well with the continuous stimulation of the deep human urge for liberation, growth, and the joy of living life together. And people live well together when they share gifts, vision, and spirituality. In this regard, then, the community called the Church as the family of God constantly needs the powerful and positive force of rebirth (i.e., continual renewal) as an increasingly sublime value. The dynamic impulse of such rebirth constantly needs to rise above pride and prejudice, complacency and fear, and divisions and greed. That is, Christian rebirth introduces and enlarges the wellspring of hope in our world. It further provides a good starting point that challenges believers to invest huge importance and prestige into playing constructive roles in giving shape to their liberating relations and destiny.

Faith and Culture Belonging Together

INTRODUCTION

WHEN READ WITHIN ITS proper perspective, experience invaluably transforms societies. Experience has no substitute. It also has no foreknowledge and no provision for hindsight. Furthermore, experience discloses and teaches that faith and culture belong to the systems of symbols.[1] And inter-human relations and dialogue about common humanity authenticate cultural differences, which ground all processes of inculturation. In fact, commonalities exist in the varying cultural practices of human existence. Similar human experiences resonate across cultures. There exists the transcendence of inevitable local values, practices, and interests of individuals and communities. By the same token, we see that beyond local social relations, interests, and ways of organizing and producing knowledge, we realize different ways of being a Christian that can be appreciated transculturally. And this fact of plural expressions of

---

1. A symbol refers to that by means of which something makes itself present and known. A symbol concretizes the presence of something that cannot be known otherwise. As a medium a symbol renders something other than itself present and actual. A symbol expresses a mode of presence of something that cannot be encountered in any other way. In this way, a symbol participates directly in the presence and power of that which it embodies without exhausting the reality. Through interaction with an interpreter a symbol makes actual the reality it embodies. While it brings into expression the reality symbolized, every interpretation of a symbol remains incomplete, inadequate, or nonexhaustive. In contrast with a symbol, a sign stands in or substitutes for something other than itself. No intrinsic relation or internal relationship exists between a sign and the reality it indicates. A sign points away from itself. See Haight, *Dynamics of Theology*, 130, 133; Schneiders, *The Revelatory Text: Interpreting the New Testament as Sacred Scripture*, 35–36.

the Christian life adds richness to the Christian faith and the missionary impulse of the Church.

The missionary character of the Church stems from the solemn command of the Lord[2] Jesus Christ:

> And Jesus came and said to them, "All authority in heaven and on earth has been given to me. Go therefore and make disciples of all nations, baptizing them in the name of the Father and of the Son and of the Holy Spirit, and teaching them to obey everything that I have commanded you. And remember, I am with you always, to the end of the age." (Matt 28:18–20)

This command of Jesus Christ continues the mission of the Son sent by the Father and the Spirit sent by the Son. The purpose of proclaiming the good news exists in the establishment and growth of the divine life in and among us through union with Christ in the Spirit. We signify and effect this purpose through lived and manifest unity by means of which we build up the humanity of others and ourselves.

The proclamation of the gospel then consists of bringing people to the knowledge and love of Jesus Christ and his message. Every proclamation and every celebration of the good news communicates Christ's liberating message of life that stimulates and nurtures meetings and gatherings that transcend differences and confrontations among people. The experience constitutes a moment of both innovation and self-evaluation, which further imply new possibilities proclaimed by words and actions. Above all, the proclamation and celebration of the good news derive their enduring lifeblood from the experience of Jesus, which always remains wonderful and assuring.

In other words, besides hope in eternal life and despite hardships, struggles, and the demands of life, the wonderful experience of Jesus brings joy and consolation in life. This is also to say that the experience, which coincides with the freedom of the spirit, brings palpable beauty and enthusiasm to concrete life. The experience of the person of Jesus continually calls us to renewed life as we give of ourselves in service to our brothers and sisters.

By virtue of the incarnation, the experience of Jesus illuminates something profound about humanity. At the same time, the human expe-

---

2. As chapter 5 will demonstrate, the lordship of Jesus de-legitimized all earthly lordship.

rience of Jesus acquires and assumes eternal value and significance. The particular meaning of the experience of Jesus, however, depends on the context of the people who participate in it. While the experience stimulates the sense of inclusiveness and flexibility, it also puts forward critiques that challenge our materialistic, social, and relational lives. In engaging the talents and gifts of people, it further provides for fuller expressions of humanity with a prophetic and critical edge. In all cases, however, the experience of Jesus enables a person or communities of persons to give a faith response to their situations, or in other words, to find joy in the midst of suffering or a constructive way of responding to life's realities. What is more, the bodily expressions and contemplative sense of life that the experience of Jesus ushers in often translate into authentic ways of being. Communal faith always nurtures and expands such an experience through care, sharing, love, and devotion of people to one another. In short, the rich experience of Jesus positively molds people's expectations, aspirations, and dreams. The experience infuses love into human interactions and creativity, which make reachable a lived sense of respect and the full life. Subsequently, continuing and reiterative graciousness, good humor, and good manners open people up to differences, a deep understanding of suffering, and commitment to people at the margins of communities or societies.

In the process of rooting oneself in the experience of Jesus Christ, a person's higher loyalty ceases to be that of convenience or expediency; it becomes loyalty to liberating and life-transforming truth. Such truth enables a person to grow and live life openly and honestly, which also means personal candor as well as the willingness to admit mistakes. The experience of liberating truth also inspires people with confidence in one another and provokes the yearning for dialogue and mediation in situations of conflict.

Obviously, we must also bear in mind that according to the Christian faith, the Jesus who walked in first-century Palestine coincides with the risen Christ of faith. We cannot separate the Jesus of history from the Jesus of faith. Jesus as human coincides with Jesus as God. The fundamental mystery of the incarnation refers to this fact. It also means that by becoming human, Christ made human dignity his own—God's own. In the person of Jesus we find the experience and expression of God's firm purpose and will. As such, then, Jesus as truly God and truly man establishes him as the savior of the world. Christ makes clear the deepest truth about God and the salvation of men and women. The divinity and humanity of Jesus authenticate the principle that God truly saved us in Christ by reconciling us with God. In this way, Christ makes it possible for us to participate in the reign of God. The Christian life of faith, then, grounds itself in a source of ultimate significance. The event of Jesus, as both man and God, implies the fact that the gospels need to be read simultaneously as works of art (history) and faith. In effect, a simply literalistic reading of the gospel cuts it short. Likewise, offering only a spiritual reading of the gospel blemishes its realism and integrity. Besides, the divinity and humanity of Jesus gives validity to the principle of coherence in interpreting the gospel. In short, an interpretation of the gospel needs to account for the various facets, meanings, and trajectories that it contains.

It thus becomes clear that the need for inculturating the Christian faith arises from the deep Christian conviction that people find and realize their salvation in the living Lord—namely, Jesus Christ. The transformation of human history and life requires an act of salvation, which has come in Christ. In other words, God's mercy, graciousness, and offer of himself in Jesus Christ actualize human redemption. In Jesus Christ, God positively and fully disposes people toward the rich life of abundant freedom. All in all, the ardor, confidence, and freedom to announce and hand on the gospel derive from the love of God in Jesus Christ. In Christ, who embodies the fullness of God's revelation, Christians see, receive, and live the fullness of God's saving act. In Christ and where Christ dwells we find the experience, expression, and communication of human plenitude, harmony, love, light, and life. In this way, Christ endows our humanity with the fullness of saving truth and eternal salvation. So the deep desire to share the good news motivates the entire thrust for continual inculturation.

When it comes to inculturation, the family sets up and forms the locus where faith and culture interact and relate very closely. In fact, many people firmly regard the family as central to their self-perception and imagination. While new contemporary possibilities, openness, and mobility alter the character of the family, family roots constantly set up and construct the searchlight by which people handle issues and approach puzzles of life. Within the nexus of the family we find a web of relationships and assumptions, values and interests, and benefits and costs that signify and actualize human agency. In this regard, some considerations of the enduring meaning of the metaphor of Church as family become apt. After all, the family fabric tends to integrate everything about life that remains open to the test of an individual life. Also, the family root goes beyond one's roots. Its scope embraces and shapes a person's world sense. It affects self-definition and with this, all of life. In this sense, the family nexus preserves and harmonizes life with enthusiasm and the joy of living. Of course, the family can also breed selfishness and insecurity. Whatever the case may be, the positive thrusts of the family inspire, enlighten, and expand the sense of self.

Within the foregoing backdrop, this chapter discusses the necessity and expands on the significance and relevance of integrating faith and culture in order that the good news touches people's lives. God comes to people through some human means of language and symbols. Of course, the task of bringing faith and culture together, or inculturation, does not come automatically even though the banquet table of life requires it. The consultative, conversational, and dialogical purpose of the process that brings together faith and culture reflects and generates new understanding, which empowers new life for believers. This process, always interpretative, illuminates the believing community when confronted with a new moment. Its illumination opens up new possibilities for human life, freedom, and action. When well done within a given cultural context, the process makes faith intelligible and faithful to Christian origins and brings forth human freedom and creativity. So, a genuine process of inculturation engages continuity with the past and newness—preservation of the original transcendent meaning and change with new perspectives.[3] Clearly, the new always depends on the old that informs it. The past must certainly be re-interpreted and contextualized so that it remains or becomes relevant. We can fulfill this task by connecting it to central human concerns and aspirations. In a certain sense, when faith remains inseparable from a converted cultural way of life of community and history it heals and transforms the brokenness of humanity from within the self, within relationships, and in the wider world.[4]

With the preceding foreword, this chapter next discusses the meaning of the family and the metaphor of the Church as family as a countervailing and transforming category. It then looks into the necessity of blending faith and culture. Thereafter, it considers the meanings of faith

---

3. Haight, *Dynamics of Theology*, 185, 187–88.
4. Gallagher, *Clashing Symbols*, 105.

and Christian faith as well as the meaning of culture. The considerations in this chapter assume that the process of bringing faith and culture together always remains multi-layered and pluralistic in its expressions, demands, and appropriateness.

THE MEANING OF THE FAMILY AND THE METAPHOR OF THE CHURCH AS FAMILY

Unity belongs to the very core of every authentic experience and expression of familyhood in spite of everything else. Decidedly, the deep cohesion of familyhood means mutual involvement in shared life and continuity. Something dramatic characterizes the assurance and experience of the family. The notion of unitary togetherness has long been wedded with that of the family, even though the family reaches out to others and the larger society. In a healthy family, we find equality of esteem and regard for all. And it exceedingly appears that in the family we talk, persuade, argue, fight with, and rely on one another as we grow, intervene in, and provide stimulus for the ebb and flow of relational warmth. Notwithstanding the challenges to its wholeness, the family seems designed to enable people to thrive both individually and in community with others. It implies commitment to solidarity, diversity, plurality, and the promotion of wellbeing of its members and neighbors. Further, basic belief in the people's capacity to remake their world and renew themselves appears to mark the thrust of family life.

In the normal and functional family, we tend to act out of love for others and with an understanding of values that we also make our own. In this way, we learn how to be attentive to others and their needs. We also grow in the habit of honoring their will and genuine desires. As we respect and promote the wellbeing of others openly and confidently we dominate and exploit them less. In the circumstances, we sow seeds of peace in which compassion does not tire. In effect, acting according to whims, caprices, chauvinism, favoritism, or cronyism becomes abusive, irksome, and hurtful to the interests of the family vitality. As a dialogical context of friendship and respect, the family thus establishes itself as a dwelling of hope where people search together for new experiences and expressions of the full life.

From a religious perspective, then, the family's emphasis on togetherness entails an enormous amount of trust that, in one sense, also symbolizes and expresses the compassion of God toward all people. So the Church as a family constitutes a milieu of relationships where we become brothers and sisters who desire to live in peace and justice. It has to do with a community rooted in God, who is experienced and shared in the world and its history of needs, sorrows, joys, and hopes.

As a countervailing and transforming metaphor, the Church as family seeks to express people's perceptions and imaginations. In this sense, it seeks to express some basic assumptions about life, the world, experience, and God. It reflects insight and a primary way of thinking and looking at reality. Further, it seeks to suggest new meanings and perspectives on the reality of Christian faith. It opens new vistas of human possibilities for interpreting life and existence. In this way, the Church as family allows for new horizons that enable us to re-imagine the social and historical reality of being the Church. This fact enables the Church to serve as a vehicle of transcendence and freedom that awakens the energies of new meanings in people's trajectories of life.

The Church as family also means that when believers approach the world from their historical context and experience, they can rediscover forgotten perspectives that make them especially alert and perhaps critical of the seemingly evident beliefs or historic achievements and trajectories of history. The Church as family symbolizes the context where generosity and courage interrelate continuously. Such a context of living lets people grow and develop simultaneously as they strive to live in harmony and unity for the common good and shared interests. Of course, this contrasts with uniformity of different interests and aspirations. Such a context implies forging common grounds as overriding values and perhaps constituting inconvenient truth, which imposes on people the sense of responsibility and interests into personal and common life. Such responsibility further makes it possible for individuals and communities to develop and flourish. It also nourishes mutual concern and goodwill that build the community as a whole. Communion of interests offers people appropriate freedom to be themselves and grow creatively. In any case, human growth, successes, accomplishments, flourishing, and fulfillment largely flow from the enrichment of multiple belongings.

Because its appeals can grip the imagination with disclosive, genuine, and admirable focus, the community of the Church as God's family frequently cannot ignore the element of sacrifice for the good of the other. The spirit of sacrifice further needs gratuity and generosity that let people know their capacities and sensibilities to improve themselves for the future. Where people employ their imagination, skills, commitment, and capacities to help each other grow, they promote each other and the experience of common life. Conversely, this perspective also means confronting hunger, thirst, nakedness, loneliness, and indignities at personal and social levels.

An active sense of the Church as family unfolds into and involves appreciation and the celebration of respect for fair treatment of all, which in turn facilitates generous and committed participation of individuals in the human community. As it were, the humanity of familyhood does not arise from the brute force of market-based circumstances. The family impulses of intimacy and closeness do not allow family members to put a gloss on cruelty, abuses, and domination, which allow some people to promote and practice degrading acts.

Accordingly, as a luminous space of acceptance, love, and healing, the Church as family exemplifies a dwelling place of mutual surrender and trust among people. In this way, it locates itself in a realm beyond advantage or merit. The Church's enormous interests in people and the fact that it possesses deep spiritual convictions establish it as a milieu without needless prerequisites and a place of embrace that directs people toward hope, light, and consolation. The equanimity of the Church as family can be likened to a huge and open gate that allows people to move toward the sanctuary of God, whose true name can only be lasting and beautiful love. God as a wellspring of love engages all thoughts, feelings, emotions, and passions with the gentle and consoling voice of truth and expansive freedom. Moreover, the whole premise of God as love stands against any form of discrimination, hatred, and wickedness.

In the concrete, however, the Church as family cannot be conceived of except as a cultural and a spiritual reality. In this regard, only when situated within the context of faith and culture do the Church's efficacy and significance come to true light. When we see the Church as family as a locus and setting for a proper understanding of faith and culture, we place ourselves in a position that enables us to appreciate it truthfully and respectably. Otherwise, we risk making euphemistic and dishonest claims about being Church in our own culture. In the process, we would fail to recognize the Church's true spiritual significance.

The claim of the Church as family takes place within the grasps of faith and culture that stand against the exigencies of bigotry, be it in the forms of racism, sexism, tribalism,[5] or caste systems. The bewilderment has been that in our times, shifting words have not reduced bigotry, which manifests itself in huge burdens of discrimination, poverty, harassment, and disparagement that many people bear. Verbal uplifts have, for the most part, effected fewer positive consequences than expected for many people beyond the etiquette and delicacy of political correctness. Beyond the words, users of verbal uplifts have often continued to wound and hurt others, without any due sense of care, regret, or remorse. In a sense, the use of verbal proprieties has largely tended to remain hollow and distasteful. They rarely translate into actual regard for the interests, concerns, and wellbeing of others. In short, verbal uplifts not incarnated into the fabric of people's lives can only represent a sterile, vacuous, and insincere contraption. It stands outside embodied cultural assumptions (which look backward) and presuppositions (which look forward).

In this way, only when we understand faith and culture well do we truly serve the truth of the Church as family. The overarching need for unity that characterizes the family cannot spring from politicization and

5. In many parts of Africa social fault lines and grievances and economic inequalities have an ethnic or tribal character to them. Ethnic chauvinism describes tribalism or properly, tribal resentment, which also often takes on territorial character. In effect, political offices, job opportunities, and allocation of public resources easily camouflage the well-cloaked practice of tribalism that runs through the fibers and fabric of socio-political life and relationships. Many politicians in Africa have perfected the art of ethnic nepotism by exploiting tribal biases to feverish pitches. This explains why in many African countries wealth and poverty have developed distinct ethnic tones. Of course, many employers hire people on the basis of merit, but frequently tribal affiliations influence or have huge bearing on an individual's access to available lucrative opportunities. The exterminatory character of tribalism gnaws away and erodes the social fabric of common life in our increasingly multi-ethnic world. It has increasingly become the troubling factor that has dogged and undermined the building of multi-tribal African communities and a common sense of nationhood in many African countries. Stifling tribal loyalties continue to determine the most blatant and tainted behaviors we find in most African settings and governance. The dishonor and stumbling block that tribalism creates make it difficult to reconstruct an active, cohesive, and a strong sense of nationhood and community. In this sense, one can speak of tribalism as the last compelling colonialist that inhibits and in some instances reverses the gains of Africa, given the fact that the contemporary concept of tribe has largely been a construct of colonialism that prospered through the practice and methods of divide and rule. The colonial divide and rule policy allotted special status to some groups while it dismissed others as of little consequence in the political dispensation. Tribalism, or more specifically, tribal resentment, continues to handicap many African peoples, organizations, and governments from pursuing clear, over-arching public goals and common transformation.

moorings of us-against-them, which itself constitutes a cul-de-sac inimical to authentic embodiment of familyhood. The metaphor of the Church as family entails much engagement and building up of human life. To these elements we must expressly add harmonious coexistence as forming the witness and seal of credibility for promising family life. At the same time, this perspective contrasts with the banal drama of optimism that grounds itself merely in image-presentation and image-management.

The Church as family implies a prevalence of open accountability and responsibility. The affirmative impulse of the Church as family acknowledges pluralism, expresses tolerance of difference, and personifies the celebration of human fraternity and brotherhood. Its effects on the human imagination imply a genuine recognition and understanding of differences of culture, history, and aspiration, which interrelate. At its core, the Church as family seeks to forge a transforming and strengthening vision that particularly answers to the needs of the weak, the aspirations of the deprived, and the demands for new cultural definitions. In this sense, the Church as family becomes emblematic of all that contrasts with, for instance, internment, torture, covert surveillance, coercion, and any form of ill-treatment. It also stands as a counter-sign to sexual and alcohol abuses, which disrupt, weaken, and destroy positive relations among people and to substance abuses, which impair good judgments. The truth of the Church as family grows and blossoms within a context of enthusiastic, generous, and tolerant collaboration between faith and culture according to circumstance, time, and place. Certainly, the passing of time can blur, change, or even erase the blend of faith and culture that historical events effect. At the same time, the Church as family does not exist without a primary discourse on God, which constitutes the subject of the next considerations.

The Church as Family and the Discourse on God

To begin, the discourse on God touches on what can bear great significance for our relationships, lives, behaviors, and activities. The notion of God implies questions of human value, worth, and self-understanding or awareness. In God, all of creation finds final meaning, purpose, and fullness. As concerned with that which could become most attractive to persons, discourse on God also engages the subject of ultimate unity of value and existence as realities of human life. Insofar as God could evoke and attract people to live well with one another, the discourse of God needs to operate within a framework of discernible transcendence, meaning, and openness.

We truly speak of the Church as a family within a primary discourse on an all-embracing God whom the Church proclaims. This God of all desires to save all and remains accessible to all. All other ecclesiological discourse (i.e., conversations concerning the Church's self-understanding), as a matter of fact, remains subordinate to God. Subsequently, conversations about the Church only follow the discourse on God. In other words, God and worship of God precede every talk about the community called the Church. The mission of glorifying God constantly guides and renews the Church. How the Church glorifies God manifests itself in the Church's prophetic and active life. Bearing and announcing the saving message of an all-embracing God is essential to the very life of the Church. Fundamentally, then, the Church's role remains one of enabling people to know and encounter God. And as the Church becomes the dwelling place of God's presence, the Church speaks of God and human kinship with a loving and liberating God. This task of the Church ends only when God truly becomes all in all—namely, when all live from God and with God. This also means that our life signifies the sacrament of the Eucharist, which symbolizes our life together and the body and blood of Christ offered up to the Father as a process of communion and oneness with God and one another.

The celebration of the Eucharist takes place in the context of the priesthood of Christ that finds its deepest meaning when understood in the light of his self-gift by the power of the Spirit in returning to the Father. In this light, the priest's identity at the celebration of the Eucharist coincides with personal participation in Christ's self-giving activity where the self-gift also represents sacrifice. In serving those entrusted to him, a priest's central and ambient roles consist of gathering the baptized assembly so that the faithful express their vocation to return the world to the Father in Christ. Of course, the cultic functions of the priesthood do not exhaust the presbyteral and sacramental character of the priestly identity and life. In other words, the power to consecrate and absolve people's sins at confessions does not encompass fully the mystery of priestly life and vocation. This fact also means, however, that the sacramental activities of the ordained priest must not be separated from other aspects of ministries like preaching and pastoral care.

Accordingly, in the celebration of the Eucharist, the welding of the divine and human communities takes place. Humanity and its world become part of God's world and vice versa. Put differently, in the celebration of the Eucharist a community of believers professes God as their Father, Christ as their brother, and the Spirit as the love that binds all the members of the community to each other. Believers come to share in God's own love and life. In the celebration of the Eucharist we find the visible embodiment of Christ himself present in our midst in the symbolic expression of unity. For the Christian Christ also symbolizes the final and definitive pattern of the true human.

It must be emphasized further that the celebration of the Eucharist exists for God before anything else. While remaining a meal, the Eucharist also has a transcendent sacrificial meaning to it. It renders the risen Christ present anew. In this way, it expresses God's intimate relationship with us and celebrates God's wish to establish an intimate connection with us in ways that always enable us to bond with one another afresh. At the Eucharistic meal and sacrifice we celebrate our sense of human and spiritual fellowship through openness to the transcendent reality of Christ in the Spirit at work in and as his body. Through the Eucharistic celebration, we renew each other; we contribute to the shaping of life as the gift of Christ through the Spirit. We then communicate abundant life. We come together in Christ who nourishes us so that we can, in turn, feed each other with life that enables joy. As a consequence, mutual creation in the Spirit of Christ takes place. The concrete reality and experience that the celebration of the Eucharist makes possible further implies increasing love for the world and the men and women in it. Eucharistically, then, the Christian vocation touches on living in, serving, and loving this world.

Or again, the Eucharistic liturgy has God as its center—that is, as an essential focus that precedes any involvement and participation of the faithful in the life of the Church. As such, appreciation of the Eucharist remains vital for the efficacious life of the Church. Authentic Eucharistic prayer breeds union and harmony among people. The valuing process enables people to form part of a community of people whom they respect and love and among whom they feel accepted and respected. The atmosphere of respect offers a sense of security, worthiness, and gentleness. In this sense, the joy of love coincides with the joy of union and harmony that communicates goodness, support, and life.

In effect, the community called the Church constantly reconstitutes itself in the celebration of the Eucharist, which implies both a deep personal relationship with God as well as face-to-face encounters with others. This dialogical character belongs to the internal nature of the Church. The Eucharistic experience reconstitutes an available communal world that recreates imagination, expectations, and the incarnate intersubjectivity (i.e., basic sense and expression of human kinship ties) of believers. However, when God ceases to be their center, liturgical experiences easily deteriorate into theatrics and loci for power struggles and ideological hegemonies.

Moreover, the Church's norms, values, practices, and expectations do well to co-mingle with all people of goodwill. In this light, the bringing together of faith and culture becomes imperative. Broadminded conversations and negotiations between faith and culture need to characterize the core of the ecclesial life. Of course, tendencies that easily lend themselves to interpretations of disloyalty or waywardness cannot be ruled out, so they may be noted and taken into account. A further challenge is one of developing symbol systems that bring together different meanings, expectations, practices, and perceptions of faith and culture. When the community of the Church internalizes specific and variegated vocabularies, attitudes, feelings, desires, roles, and basic moves of culture and faith, the Church forges a new interpretation of the social world. Putting faith and culture in continuous dialogue co-produces a new social world. And this new cohesive order brings with it exposure, limitation, and demands that come with particular contexts and ways of being Church.

INCULTURATION AND EVANGELIZATION

Inculturation and the Embodiment of God's Presence

According to the Christian faith, only God can save the world, and Jesus epitomizes God's way of doing that in a finite and historical personal life. In this sense, Jesus Christ demonstrates and symbolizes God's commitment to save the world. Christ represents God's salvific work. Christ symbolizes best God's ways of laboring, working, and giving of himself in love and thanksgiving in unassuming and ordinary ways. This also means that, in a real sense, we cannot be Christians without faith understood as a life lived absolutely out of a personal and communal relationship to Jesus

Christ and his message. When a daily act of orientation in faith places us before Christ, we grow in freedom, availability, and creativity.

In Jesus we find the unsurpassable pattern of God acting in history and in the world for salvation. But the local history of Jesus does not set the final determination of where, when, and under what circumstances God acts for salvation. The local historical definition of the power that saves can be found in many settings and under multiple dimensions. This is also to say that we do not at any given moment grasp the entirety of God's saving work in the world. In other words, no single culture exhausts the saving reality of Christ. We cannot confine or control the redemptive work of God in Jesus of Nazareth to a particular culture. God's ways remain hidden yet ubiquitous and hence somewhat elusive, time-bound, and contextual. Many dimensions of human experience, achievement, weaknesses, and failures need the light of Christ. This fact represents to us the promise, challenge, invitation, and call to go forward with the process of inculturation.

Inculturation as a process, then, bears a transformative significance. It translates into the language of the people the saving event wrought by Jesus as God-man. In this sense, inculturation enacts, realizes, celebrates, and embodies God's saving presence in the concrete life of the people. Of course, the process of inculturation always involves taking risk and not giving up our faith and cultural convictions. It implies letting ourselves be called into question in a new way so that we may live a fuller, more concrete life. After all, both faith and culture respond to the enigmas of the human condition interactively and dialogically. When faith and culture do not simply tolerate but also encounter each other we arrive at collaboration and dialogue between the two that takes into account the joys and troubles of living. The spiritual and moral heritage of faith and culture frequently provides values that consolidate hope and the common good necessary for harmonious society.

Inculturation always remains a give-and-take process. Mutual understanding and mutual enrichment between faith and culture constitute the express goals of the exchange that characterizes all of its processes. This also means, however, that eclectic, selective, and arbitrary approaches to local contexts do not provide an effective way of engaging local cultures. The spirit and function of inculturation serve to connect local practices and pragmatic interests with nourishing faith and hope.

Faith and Culture Belonging Together

Of course, as we undertake the process of inculturation we have to understand the Church's interpretation of culture and culture's interpretation of the Church in light of its ongoing and open self-understanding. Since evangelization needs to help people hear about the living Christ as well as encounter him, inculturation provides for a renewal of faith. It gives fresh vitality to the life-giving and enduring word of God—hope for peace, justice, and freedom, which summon all to responsibility, cultivation of virtue, and discipline. These sublime qualities of the Christian calling make possible reconciliation, healing, and love to all as brothers and sisters of the same quality.

In the Garden of Faith and Culture

Christianity remains profoundly social, in that it always seeks to become culture—namely, to create and foster a culture of human flourishing. The reason lies in the fact that when the gospel finds a dwelling place in the social and cultural order, it makes a powerful contribution to the common or public good. This also means that people's basic impulses can find adequate expression when the gospel and culture engage each other constructively. Often, unspoken aspirations that people nurture touch on the sources and shared values that nourish people's spiritual and religious sense. In this way, the richness and newness of the gospel in different contexts of life require ongoing processes of adaptation and reincarnation.

In the context of Christian faith, as already pointed out earlier, Christ came to save and free humankind by re-orienting their hopes and their aspirations, their struggles and their sufferings, and their successes and their failures. The salvation and freedom that Christ brings implies faith lived out in a cultural context. We do not live our lives outside our bodies that place us in history and cultures. Of course, while rooted in the heart, the redemption and liberation that faith engenders remain spiritual and interior before expressing themselves ecstatically in the practical world. This also means that the life-giving Spirit wells up and refreshes us within actual cultural exigencies.

Culture lies at the root of identities, human intercommunication, and creativity. It shapes the interior sense that people have as being self-conscious and self-determining in living life with others. In many ways, then, culture strengthens, concentrates, and clarifies the personal voice, character, and roles of individuals as they interact with their world.

In spite of everything, a person often reveals himself or herself in a dramatic cultural context through the interplay of the presence and absence of others, which implies a person's dialogue with his or her physical and social worlds. In this sense, people always remain adaptive and creative. Fundamentally, people tend to reach beyond themselves as they interrelate with their world. Existentially, this means that the uniqueness of human personalities exists in their embodied narratives, continuing consciousness, and self-awareness within a given historical, cultural context. This frequently entails freedom and openness to shared judgment, accountability, and social response.

As expressing internal and external as well as personal and group identities, culture deals with and shapes behaviors, language, and problem-solving approaches to existence. It also involves ideas, beliefs, construction of meaning, and norms of behavior. Within this framework, religion remains deeply cultural; that is, it reveals itself as a mode of cultural behavior. In any case, people experience God through cultural images, concepts, and expressions. In effect, Christianity can only express itself meaningfully in cultural ways and terms. Thus, the material and functional expressions of Christianity cannot simply be considered less important than the spiritual aspects, which include faith, beliefs, values, worship, and morality.

Without a doubt, then, a dynamic relationship exists between the Christian message and culture. This relationship can assume positive forms of reciprocal and critical (questioning) interactions and interpretations. But real barriers also threaten a fruitful interchange between Christian faith and culture. First, we have the barrier of the fear of change. People usually do not like to change their attitudes, lifestyles, and patterns of behavior. Second, we have the barrier of ignorance. We only love what we know so that when we do not know and love something, we cannot appropriate it or make it a part of our life. This further means that in order to change our attitudes and behaviors we need knowledge. Third, we have the barrier of prejudice, which stems from ignorance and malice and the refusal to submit to the critiques of lived experience. Malice signifies that a person delights in and celebrates the suffering and pain of another. Frequently, prejudice leads to systematic discrimination, which institutes unexamined habits or the practice of injustice. Nevertheless, inculturation signifies the transmission of a system of meanings, beliefs, values, and customs of one culture into another. Creative communication, as expressive of living activity and practice between faith and culture, needs to lead to some living relations between these two basic aspects of existence.

Come what may, faith does not cancel out culture, and culture does not cancel out faith. Seen from this standpoint, Christian faith and culture need to relate to each other continuously, positively, and creatively. In different yet complementary ways, Christian faith and culture together enhance greater apprehension and appreciation of the truth of humanity. Within the framework of humanity, the primary question of Christianity coincides with the question of truth, which makes unavoidable claims on us and which make us present to ourselves and our world.

Put differently, faith and culture link people together in life. In the context of Christianity, when faith and culture come together fruitfully, they facilitate a more authentic, convinced, and convincing way of living the Christian faith or the gospel. Their positive blend helps Christians embody the vocation of discipleship in the daily facets of their lives—that is, at home, at work, at leisure, in sports, and around the neighborhood. In actual fact, the missionary demand that follows from Christian disciple-ship carries with it the mandate to evangelize in ways that honor and safeguard the freedom and dignity of persons and cultures.

In a sense, then, faith and culture enable people to express and real-ize their basic longing for fulfillment, definitive liberation, or quest for the fullness of life. In many ways, both faith and culture express forms of life-giving illuminations, notwithstanding the lopsidedness that their expressions may give on account of human contingency and historicity. While culture naturally tends to prefigure, herald, and typify human at-tempts at reaching out to a fuller meaning from beginning to end, we find inbuilt in faith liberative energies that seek to realize the very presence of God's kingdom in this world.

A grounding theological belief for bringing faith and culture togeth-er lies in the conviction that the Spirit of God already exists and operates in all cultures. This also means that we cannot confine God to our hu-man categories and myths. This fact provides an opening for constructive engagement between faith and culture. While by no means obvious, we can discern positive glimpses of God's reality in cultures. In a sense, no culture exists without God's presence and activities, which always remain life-giving. After all, according to Christian faith, God remains the creator of all so that Christianity, in one sense, simply makes explicit the fact of God's closeness and relationship with creation through various cultures.

Within this understanding, Christian faith affirms the common humanity of all; it regards all with esteem and respect.

The universality of the Spirit gives rise to reverence for goodness present in cultures as well as the discernment of grace in the lived values and symbols of peoples. In other words, there exist people who do not formally belong to the Church, yet who do God's work in spirit and truth. Furthermore, at the heart of Christian faith one finds evangelization that requires mutual engagement and enrichment between faith and culture. This means that evangelization entails the quest for appropriate languages of faith in meeting the spiritual sensibilities of cultures. The gospel becomes a concrete reality in the lives of men and women only when they receive, feel, celebrate, and live it in the language and sensitivities of local cultures.[6] Within this perspective, culture and faith can be seen as expressing God's continuing relationship with us in our responsibility for the earth, for each other, and for human history itself. The positive elements of faith and culture together express the human response to God's continuing creative gift in human freedom and responsibility.[7]

Indeed, the coming of Christ radically justifies the blending of faith and culture. The birth, growth, and life of the earthly Jesus happened in a given culture at a given time. In this sense, then, he ordained cultures and set a primordial example for joining culture and faith together. In Christ, God clothes himself in flesh and converses and interacts with cultural people. Through the incarnation, then, God not only became matter, but he also inhabited matter and worked out human salvation through it within the exigencies of a particular culture. Through the incarnation, God illuminated and took form in cultural embodiment; Jesus spoke a cultural language and used cultural images in his ministry, works, and ways of speaking about God. When God took fleshly form in the person of Jesus Christ, he blessed the whole realm of culture and made it a fitting instrument for birthing forth and manifesting the divine splendor. He reclaimed every culture as a vehicle for his service. Everyday cultural life, thus, can become an enlivening means by which people glorify God and receive the grace of the Holy Spirit. In this light, inculturation imitates, so to speak, the embracing of humanity by God in Christ, in order to give flesh to the gospel again in different cultures.

---

6. Ibid., 104.

7. Ibid., 105.

The incarnation took place in history in clearly defined circumstances of time and space—that is, amidst people with their own cultures.[8] The more human we live, the more divine we actually become since by the incarnation Jesus showed us how to live life in an abundant way that holds us together and leads us to God.

Evidently, Christian faith lives in a world of sounds, images, colors, impulses, and vibrations, all of which receive their forms from cultural categories and traditions. And tradition includes everything significant in the present and as described by different voices. It assigns importance to different perspectives, capabilities, and responses to present states of affairs. On the basis of the pervasive influence of traditions, the gospel faith demands, for its relevance, embodiment in the traditions and customs of various cultures through proclamation. People receive and welcome the word of God after they hear it and realize that it embodies the presence and power of God in ways that appeal to them culturally. Commonly, such a reception also stimulates a spirit of generosity and communion in people who receive God's word. As an essential part of the Christian faith, then, proclamation becomes effective when it reaches the many dimensions of human life: religious and spiritual, moral and ethical, physical and environmental, political and economic, and cultural and educational.

Additionally, proclamation needs to extend from individuals to families, communities, nations, and the regions of the world. This extension implies being attentive to situations and particular cultural visions. Sharing the good news with children, youth, adults, men and women, workers and employers, leaders and servants, refugees and displaced people, and the disadvantaged and handicapped requires the coupling of faith and cultural forms and experiences whose expanse reaches the entirety of life. Thus, the inculturation of the Christian message arises out of the necessity of making the Christian faith relevant to all times, circumstances, and peoples. Indeed, Christianity cannot but express itself in some vivid cultural forms.[9]

When culture and faith hang together and achieve harmony, they make possible effective and contextualized proclamation of the Christian faith. In order to explain the meaning of God's word in a way that relates to the lives of the people, the good news needs to be interpreted in

8. Ibid., 106.
9. Ibid., 103.

terms understandable to particular historical and cultural contexts. The proclamation of the Christian faith needs to be sensitive to the cares, concerns, needs, and fortunes of the people faith seeks to reach so that it truly refreshes their lives. It remains significant, then, to recognize that the emergence of a healthy relationship between faith and culture truly bases itself on love, care, mutual respect, honesty, shared interests, and truth. In other words, a wholesome relationship between faith and culture must not be merely based on consolidation of commercial interests, political expediency, or an ideological scramble for power and wealth.

Only a contextualized or inculturated faith challenges credibly cultural patterns of disordered affections and habits that may stifle healthy growth of individuals and communities. Faith needs to challenge elements of social fragmentation, greed, and indifference to human suffering that a culture may foster. In this regard, we may note that the exigency (which means need and demand simultaneously) and resources of faith may rightly challenge cultural tendencies of, say, racism, sexism, tribalism, ethnocracy, social ostracism, classicism, and bigotry, as well as pharisaical hypocrisy. The exigency of faith cannot be indifferent to concrete issues that pertain, for example, to HIV/AIDS and health care, displaced persons, and unjust structures of a given society. In the midst of life, Christianity does not simply preoccupy itself with vague, benign generalities. In other words, Christianity needs to touch and leaven every concrete aspect of human life and relationships. Nothing in a culture need be foreign to an inculturated faith. An inculturated faith infuses all of life with its rays of self-pacification. It also enhances the growth of individuals and communities in a spirit of hope and love. An inculturated Christian faith constantly strives to transcend narrow individual and collective cultural interests by promoting and expanding a sense of the common good.

What is more, an inculturated faith can meaningfully challenge a given culture to greater openness so that it becomes less violent or hostile to the creative gifts that people bring to this life. A truly inculturated faith promotes growth in just living and affectionate respect for all people. A sensibility that faith brings to a culture might encourage the sharing of resources and the physical supports of life. Also, faith may illumine a given culture by inspiring care for the poor and the oppressed or promoting unity and collaboration and union among diverse groups. Certainly,

Christian faith cherishes and promotes repentance, reconciliation, forgiveness, and kindness.

The history of Christian faith, too, could be said to be one involving faith and culture together, beginning with Jesus, who fitted his teaching and ministry with the Jewish religious ethos and traditions. A lot of Christian practices emerged and developed from Judaism. This also means that Christian identity coincides with a certain contextual way of life. The New Testament times witnessed vibrant moments of incorporating the Jews and gentiles, the Christian faith and the Hellenistic culture. The process entailed a lot of continuities and discontinuities. Christianity links itself closely with historical persons and action—namely with the profound experience of Jesus and the apostolic witnesses. In this way, the Christian message constantly requires interpretations and re-interpretations. In fact, Christianity as it expanded in the West and in North Africa in the early centuries inculturated itself differently. So, inculturation from the Christian perspective has always been ongoing right from its beginnings. Further, inculturation seeks to echo the miracle of unity and diversity at Pentecost, which involved an extraordinary reaching out and acceptance into a variety of languages of diverse cultures. It belongs to the very character of the Christian faith itself to mold culture and to let itself be molded by culture. We need inculturation in order to live our faith well according to contexts and time. If cultures need Christ for their fullness, Christ needs cultures in order to continue and complete the gift of the incarnation in different contexts of history.[10] A certain kinship binds together faith and culture in the human spiritual itinerary to an ever-fuller life.

UNDERSTANDING FAITH

Faith and Transcendence

In the first place, religion has always been an important feature of human life, individually, communally, interpersonally, and organizationally. Religion offers people a transcendent (i.e., enlarged and rounding) frame of orientation and object of devotion that shapes and motivates them to be and act in purposeful and consistent ways. What is more, what motivates us defines and organizes our impressions and strivings in existence.

10. Ibid., 107–8.

The object of devotion forms and sets up the basis for human affective values and valuations. Every society appears to nurture and observe some form or sort of religious beliefs. In other words, religion plays a very important part in the lives of many people as an active system that affects their interpretation and their understanding of life and the world. In one sense, thus, religion seems to connect very closely and coincide with the need and demand of human life itself.

In effect, religion contains much meaning and significance for various kinds of people. We have a number of religious beliefs with which people negotiate their existence. What is more, faith forms a central experience and nexus in religious thought and actions or activities. Faith occupies a central place in people's religious life. This is also to say that many people in this world live by faith. In particular, faith appears to relate uniquely to religions in which there exists some form of worship. In this respect, the experience of faith marks itself by some reverential devotion to something transcendent or divine. Subsequently, the deep demand for a transcendent frame of reference marks all human religious quests for fulfilling truth, enlivening goodness, and surpassing beauty. In fact, authentic religiosity aids the unfolding of specifically human powers and answers the human need for purposeful life or meaning in life. Excepting their concrete details, religious experiences and expressions often take on ritualistic, conceptual, and institutional forms.

Admittedly, then, people live by faith on account of their religious sensibility. In this regard, faith expresses the human experience of, and connection with, transcendence that coincides with God. In one sense, thus, we cannot separate faith from some forms of human awareness, inquiry, and discovery. Because many people live by it, faith accompanies many people as a constitutive and dynamic element of the human. When faith is genuinely religious and attaches itself to an object that always remains transcendently ultimate, it has its object revealed to it. People receive faith through revelation. In this light, then, faith signifies and guides the unveiling and manifestation of the object of faith to human consciousness.[11] Also, we cannot separate faith from an act and commitment of freedom. And the authority of faith coincides ultimately with God's authority recognized within an experience of a religious encounter. In faith, we find

---

11. Haight, *Dynamics of Theology*, 51.

self-authentication of religious experience.[12] What is more, the object of faith reveals itself only when we respond to its self-communication or self-manifestation.[13]

As spiritual beings, people can commit themselves in faith with a determination and a definition that includes their total selves. In this sense, faith centers people. The commitment of faith implies acting in a stable and consistent manner by clinging to symbols, truths, and values that give meaning and coherence to human existence at its most fundamental levels. For this reason, faith engages the loyalty and commands the whole of the human personality in a central and centering way. Furthermore, faith always focuses on human salvation. Hence, faith asks the following question: what objects, values, or supreme reality require absolute dedication and commitment proper to a fuller expression of human freedom? Faith reaches out from the depths of human freedom, which engages all human energies and powers. In this regard, faith unifies and holds together all aspects of the human personality.[14] After all, the object of commitment of faith transcends the self and exalts freedom itself.[15] In its existential reality, then, faith manifests and reflects the actual human reaction and response to freedom.

As noted, the object of faith transcends the finitude of this world and everything in it taken together. Hence, faith exists when one accepts and receives a transcendent value and actually surrenders one's life to it in committed loyalty. Faith really exists in the actual surrender and dedication to a value that constitutes a person's life.[16] In other words, the ultimate object of faith coincides with the one in whom we believe—namely, the living presence and action of God in and through this life. The object of authentic religious faith disposes the human subject toward the transcendent even though faith always entails some relationship with the reality of this world. Without the transcendence of its object, the faith in question cannot be said to be religious in the proper sense.[17] The object of faith reveals itself to a person who experiences it as from *above*. In this sense,

12. Ibid., 104.
13. Ibid., 52.
14. Ibid., 20.
15. Ibid., 19.
16. Ibid., 29.
17. Ibid., 22.

faith may be spoken of as a gift of God as Spirit.[18] In addition, faith interacts with human wishes and imagination. When faith interprets its object well, it interprets the world well. In this regard, faith affects how persons live their lives in this world, individually and interactively. Faith cannot exist without beliefs about its object of faith—namely, without objective characterizations in language of the object of faith.

Of course, beliefs change and need to change as faith commitments allow for different interpretations and expressions. In this regard, expressions of beliefs always remain partial, fragmentary, limited, relative, and incomplete. Subsequently, faith always coexists with some set of ideologies. This means that faith in a transcendent reality cannot exist without imaginative portrayals of its object, interpretations of its object, propositions about the transcendent reality, and interpretations of the finite world in the light of transcendence.[19]

The object of faith impacts the logic and interior momentum of people's behaviors and relationships. The commitment of faith bears itself out in action. Faith carries with it a dimension of praxis. But only extended reflective analysis of faith brings to awareness its embeddedness in human life. The object of a person's real faith lies in the radical orientation of a person at any given time and circumstance. This orientation reveals itself through the sum total of concrete decisions that make up a person's character and life. Faith connects closely with human action that constitutes and manifests it. In a certain sense, faith involves the dynamic commitment of the entire person in action. Faith reveals its object through the actions and activities it inspires and that guide and direct a person's life and aspirations.[20] In this light, faith shares inevitably and inescapably in the public sphere because the nature of faith concerns the ultimate truth of human beings, human activities, and human relationality. The ultimate nature of faith makes it public. The desire for fullness of human truth demonstrates the inbuilt tendency of faith to communicate itself in concrete forms.[21]

---

18. Ibid., 24.
19. Ibid., 27.
20. Ibid., 29–30.
21. Ibid., 33.

Faith and Belief

The necessity by which faith expresses itself in beliefs makes faith public. When people publicly communicate their religious beliefs, they create and form a community of faith. When the experience and the expression of faith become public they also frequently imply some alignment with particular convictions and traditions. Furthermore, the community shapes, forms, and fashions the faith of an individual through its belief system and actions that vitally express it.[22] A given faith expression integrates, shares, enters into, and participates in some vital tradition through active involvement.

The forms in which beliefs exist and people express them change with time and contexts. Beliefs always change to new forms as they seek new definitions, symbols, images, and words in order to remain relevant. As symbols and words change, so do beliefs develop. People constantly change their lives. The priority of faith over beliefs, then, implies the priority of the personal over all secondary institutional forms and ideological expressions.

The community of faith frequently anchors its identity on some beliefs expressed through shared symbols, beliefs, values, and doctrines that extend into the far past. So, a person's most personal belief also becomes necessarily social and hence, cultural. In this way, faith becomes a public act and an attitude that implies co-responsibility with the communities of other people. To have faith implies belonging to an extended community and a vital sacred tradition.[23] The faith of a believing community expresses itself in its corporate beliefs, behavior, and actions in the world. The praxis of the beliefs shows in the community's concrete concerns and historical demands or needs. The praxis of faith means that a living faith cannot be indifferent to human misery and suffering, oppression and death, marriage and social relations among people, or environmental concerns.

Faith and Revelation

In the first place, revelation refers to God making himself known to human beings in history. The meaning of revelation coincides with the event of God's self-communication in history that continues to the present. As God's free self-expression to humans, revelation connects

22. Ibid.
23. Ibid., 34.

intimately with faith. People receive revelation through faith. And the experience of revelation coincides with God as creative Spirit, namely, God as impacting the world, especially in human lives. Or again, God present and active in creation coextends with God as Spirit, who presents himself to human personhood and freedom.[24] As an existential experience of transcendence, revelation enables people to recognize and understand that the confines of religious traditions do not circumscribe all experiences. Revelation as a consciousness of God's presence exists as something potentially available to all.[25] In revelation, God really becomes present to and enters into real dialogue with people. But some finite historical medium always mediates this dialogue. And such mediums grasp and connect with human wishes, imagination, and contemplation. This fact further implies that human consciousness contains within itself a dynamism that makes understanding the experience and feelings of transcendence possible.[26] In effect, in interpreting the content of revelation that gives rise to faith, one needs to make a distinction between the medium that mediates God's presence and the objective interpretations of God to which the medium may give rise.[27]

As such, revelation develops and changes. God revealing himself and being revealed to vital human experiences occur in ever-new ways. Revelation as developing also implies original revelation, which refers to the first occurrence of a particular revelation. In other words, the original and originating experience of God's presence in a specific way through a historical medium stands at the head of a religious tradition.[28] In fact, revelation informs, animates, and transforms human existence in this world both individually and socially.

The gap between authentic experience of transcendence and the received memories that people interpret, codify, formalize, and institutionalize in beliefs can become a real chasm between honesty and hypocrisy. The possibility and reality of hypocrisy underlie the religious practice of every long, rich, and complex tradition. Creedal statements and religious experiences do not always match. They can lead to complacent piety and

24. Ibid., 59.
25. Ibid., 60.
26. Ibid., 63.
27. Ibid., 67.
28. Ibid., 81.

intolerant self-righteousness, which in turn can cause much protracted suffering and guilt. At the same time, the gap between creedal statements and authentic religious experience offers the opportunities for human growth and development if acknowledged and interpreted honestly. In short, religious traditions retain their aliveness and spiritual verve if they demand that creedal statements constantly root themselves in experiences that call persons and human relations to a certain fullness of life. Human beings do not merely achieve this fullness of life; rather, they accept and realize it through particular judgments, choices, and activities.

Faith and Ultimate Concern

Thus far, faith refers to the ultimate concerns of man and woman. Ultimate concern coincides with passionate concern; it involves an infinite concern that exalts and directs human freedom to its fulfillment. Just like any other, such passion always entails some bodily basis.[29] In other words, an act of faith pertains to a finite body being grasped by and turned to the infinite.[30] In this respect, passionate concern not only refers to the unconditional demand made by one's ultimate concern; it also signifies the promise of ultimate fulfillment accepted in the act of faith.[31] The unconditional concern, such as faith, points toward the ultimate concern.[32] Ultimate concern motivates a person passionately, totally, and completely in terms of giving him or her final meaning, justification, and significance in existence. The object of ultimate concern grasps consciousness in terms perceived and understood as a plenitudinous transcendent value. Connecting with ultimate concern, then, constitutes a cherished central organizing vision and leitmotif of life itself. Ultimate concern engages the centered act of the personality, which includes the total surrender to its content.[33] As an act of ultimate concern, faith engages the total person so that it always deeply touches on the matter of personal and existential freedom.[34]

In addition, faith reaches out ecstatically toward saving truth. Within the ecstasy of faith we find and experience an awareness of liberating truth

29. Tillich, *Dynamics of Faith*, 106.

30. Ibid., 16.

31. Ibid., 2.

32. Ibid., 9.

33. Ibid., 25.

34. Ibid., 5.

and ethical value. In effect, cognitive affirmation and an emotional experience accompany every movement of faith.[35] Moreover, the person who enters the sphere of faith awakens to the sanctuary of life and holiness. This also means that the awareness of the holy or the sacred coincides with an awareness of the presence of the divine mystery. In every case, ecstatic attraction and fascination manifest and abide in mystery.[36] The holy, always experienced as present, grasps the mind and personality with terrifying and fascinating power. It represents, in a sense, what we essentially are and ought to be.[37] The experience also means that the creative character of the divine constantly seeks victory over the destructive forces of life. In the experience of the holy, the ontological and the moral elements clasp hands and unite.[38]

Besides, the uncertainty that attends every act or movement of faith points to the fact that the finite always receives and relates inadequately with the infinite. Or again, the element of uncertainty in faith cannot be removed.[39] In other words, existential doubt accompanies every act, experience, and expression of faith. Conversely, serious doubt confirms faith. It continually indicates and confirms the unconditional character of faith's concern. Uncertainty about the living mystery of God or the transcendent marks the human condition. We cannot conceptually pin down God. We can only bear witness to God in our lives. Witnesses of prayer, service, and life provide effective pointers to the living mystery of the God of unlimited love. People learn about and experience God's unlimited love through friendships, quality of family life, and communion of men and women, namely through cultural expressions that honor life and its positive expressions that mediate the sense of transcendence. In the end, it becomes increasingly evident that the experiences and manifestations of ultimate concern carry with them vital risks and the courage to fully become oneself.[40]

35. Ibid., 7.
36. Ibid., 13.
37. Ibid., 56.
38. Ibid., 69.
39. Ibid., 16.
40. Ibid., 18.

Faith and Freedom

Faith grows in freedom to the extent that it takes God alone as its motive. The freedom of faith bears reference to truth. It directs itself toward truth as the dwelling place of life in abundance. In this sense, the freedom of faith derives from grace, where grace stands for God's own self-manifestation. We apprehend God's grace through its holy effects, which include interior light, consolation, and a sense of union with God. Of course, the freedom of faith may be limited in particular cases by social and psychological pressures of the believer.[41] Normally, the response of faith comes from the external word of proclamation even though interior self-communication with God always remains a part.[42] People grow in faith in as much as they advance in explicit knowledge of the contents of revelation and trust more in God's mercy and goodness. They also grow in faith as they turn more to God himself as the sole motive for believing and the sole source of true security in life. Hence, the spiritual gifts of wisdom, understanding, and knowledge bring faith to its full stature.[43] For the Christian, faith reaches its full and divinely intended stature and fullness of freedom in Christ. Or again, Jesus brings to completion the movement of sacred history. The whole patterns of sacred history hold together in Jesus Christ, in whom they reach their summit and consummation.[44] Christian faith consists of a free and warm welcome of the good news of what God has done for humanity in Christ.[45]

Faith faces challenges when persons come to place their final trust in natural forces, military and political power, wealth, and other created agencies or spurious revelations. Other factors of life that imperil faith include secularism, erosion of sociological supports, the rapidity of cultural changes, the aggressive propaganda of alternative belief systems, and the bewildering variety of contemporary options.[46]

41. Ibid., 275.
42. Ibid., 277.
43. Ibid., 278.
44. Ibid., 280.
45. Ibid., 281.
46. Ibid., 279.

Faith and the Christian Perspective

In Christianity, God became a human being in Jesus Christ who charts and guides basic Christian assumptions and interpretations of being, life, and the world. So, Christian faith stresses the centrality of the living figure of Jesus. His figure illuminates all Christian sensibilities, imagery, and imagination. The person of Jesus reveals pre-eminently the person of God. All Christian media then relate to Jesus as the absolute center of the mediation of Christian truth. They either derive from him or relate back to him for their peculiar Christian meaning and authenticity.[47] Jesus mediates the experience of God as personal and infinitely caring love. He called and related to God as Father.[48] In this regard, Jesus defines the Christian imagination and the Christian concept of God. Accordingly, the New Testament preserves the figure of Jesus of Nazareth as the central medium of Christian revelation. The matter of God's self-disclosure in and through Scripture in the person of Jesus remains fundamental to the full grasp and adequate confession of the authority of Christian faith and praxis. Certainly, this fact does not preclude God's self-disclosure in and through nature.

Without the figure of Jesus, Christian revelation would not exist, strictly speaking. His figure brings together and unifies the whole of the Bible. In this light, the New Testament writings maintain a unity insofar as they all reflect and embrace the Christian experience of God in Jesus. The New Testament continues and extends the teaching and presence of Jesus. That Jesus establishes the historical medium of Christian revelation implies both Jesus's own experience of God as well as being a subject of revelation.[49] The deeper journey of the Christian faith thus takes a person into the realization that this life has its authentic roots in the life of God and cannot be separated from it.

What is more, Jesus can be understood transculturally. His message and the content of revelation that he mediated have universal and transcultural meaning and relevance. The God revealed in Jesus creates and embraces all. Jesus revealed a personal, forgiving, and boundlessly loving God of all. The God that Jesus reveals has no ethnic, racial, geographical, or tribal particularity. This God relates through God's acts in history as the

47. Ibid., 71.
48. Ibid., 85.
49. Ibid., 98–99.

God of the universe. In the end, the authority of Scripture holds when and only insofar as it mediates an encounter with God.[50] The ordinary fruits of awe, humility, realism, and joy well up from a human encounter with God. The revelation of God in and through Jesus means that God works in Jesus Christ in some final and eschatological way. A true, decisive self-communication of God to the human race takes place in Jesus. In point of fact, then, no authentic revelation of God contradicts the revelation of God in Jesus.[51]

Faith draws the Christian into the ever-expanding self-knowledge of God in Jesus. This process of incorporation into the inner life of God enables Christians to achieve a common consciousness and a bond in the single ground of being. The Christian comes to truly know himself or herself and others in Jesus. In this knowledge further exists the mutual commitment to the unconditional value, uniqueness, and lovableness of each person and set of kinship ties among people. In it we also find an unconditional acceptance of *our* inalienable communion that transforms the mundane into a world of meaning and mystery radiant with a light that originates from deep within human freedom and spirit. Faith thus sets up the precondition and provides the frame for the communication of personal reality. In a real sense, Christian faith that fills and sustains the Christian continually refers to Jesus himself. This faith corresponds to the supreme meaning and authentication of a Christian's life as well as responsibilities for his or her existence and harmonious coexistence with others. The faith of the Christian carries resonance that coheres with the consciousness of Jesus. Christian faith harmonizes with Jesus, who continually lives in agreement with God as the source of the wonder of our being.

From the Christian perspective, faith remains a gift of God unconditionally esteemed and trusted, loved and believed, and obeyed. Faith involves self-surrender to God, who reveals himself in Jesus Christ. So faith embodies a single complex reality having different aspects in which assent, trust, obedience, and loving self-communication interweave. In faith, God reveals himself as teacher or enlightener, merciful benefactor or lover, revered ruler or great emancipator, or as the ever-blessed source of life. God has placed within the human heart a restlessness that can-

---

50. Ibid., 103.
51. Ibid., 106–7.

not be appeased except by God's loving presence and self-manifestation. God calls people to participate in his own divine life so that faith will take root at the deepest level of the human personality. In this sense, faith transforms believers on the interior as it orients them toward God as Creator, Savior, and last end. Through faith, people respond to revelation of God and enter into a saving relationship with him.[52]

On the whole, the proper and compelling object of faith carries with it human meaning and future, which afford and increase the existentiality (experiential reason) of the believer. This also means that God as the object of faith corresponds to utter worth, which breeds wholeness, harmony, and fulfillment in our often distorted and broken personal and communal lives. In its continuity, then, faith enriches life with the terms of ultimate reality and meaning. The intuitive power of faith integrates and guides our human reality with truth, illuminations, and assurance. Within this perspective, the capacity and experience of the spiritual inspire us to reflect continually on the significance and relevance of human life within particular contexts. When faith does not become a mere motivating fascination, it bears with it attributive significance. In fact, through faith we gain insight into the structure of the continually evolving human meaning. Ultimately, we cannot separate God from the narratives that inspire and shape human experiences.

UNDERSTANDING CULTURE

Culture has both historical and political dimensions. Politically, the concept of culture can be used to advance political aims or achieve political purposes. Historically, we can use the concept of culture to speak about beliefs, practices, and action-oriented systems of meanings that specify a group or community of persons. In this light, we can use the concept of culture to refer to a standard of cultivation and accomplishment, as when people speak of someone as "cultured." In all its variety of understanding, culture affects how people understand themselves, what ideas and values have effects on their relationships, and what they do and how they do what they do. Culture, then, comprehends an entire life of a community and individuals. Even knowledge, in this regard, presents itself as a product or feature of particular cultural heritages. After all, culture provides the categories by which people sort out, select, choose, and adapt attitudes,

52. Dulles, *Assurance of Things Hoped For*, 180–81, 274–75.

outlooks, and institutions that they build up and whatever elements of existence they consider important and worthwhile.

Not less importantly, then, culture denotes a historically and relationally transmitted pattern of meanings embodied in symbols. Culture continually forges and produces a system of inherited conceptions expressed in symbolic forms. Men and women use these symbolic forms to communicate, perpetuate, and develop their understanding, relationships, and attitudes toward life as a whole.[53] Indeed, culture embraces an over-arching value system and vision of a society. As a multi-layered and highly differentiated reality, culture offers historical and descriptive accounts of life and also contains certain normative elements that influence life. Culture frequently manifests itself in a given set of behaviors that bear all kinds of symbolic significance. Underlying visions and beliefs, stability and dependency inform various cultural expectations and control. In providing a structure for living together and organizing relations among people, culture plays a formative role in people's lives.[54]

As embedded in a whole range of activities and practices, the common sense of a society forms part of its culture. Culture, however, does not lend itself to a simple definition; the notion covers a complex reality that provides the ambient reality for every concrete human existence. Basic visions and beliefs, rooted in various forms of social expectations and control, produce different trajectories in a culture. Undoubtedly, immediate surroundings refine the distribution of the various elements within a culture. Nature's diverse configurations provide for distinctive cultural regularities and cultural interests, cultural metaphors and cultural narratives, and the community's internal procedures.

Obviously, culture establishes the general locus of common meanings and values, customs and practices, work habits and traditions, and the spirit of questioning the data of experience. In this sense, we could say of culture that its ethos informs and arises from varying forms of human associations and of organizing human life. A given culture tends to provide people with assumptions and tools for interpreting and living life in proven manners and terms. From a religious point of view, diverse cultures have different senses of divine transcendence and the possibil-

---

53. Geertz, *Interpretation of Cultures*, 89.
54. Gallagher, *Clashing Symbols*, 14–15.

ity of arriving at religious commitment.[55] So, we may regard culture as a place of celebrating human transcendence and of creative encounters with God or the divine transcendence.[56] In this light, faith and culture intersect intimately.

Cultural symbolic forms represent express means by which people communicate, perpetuate, and develop their understanding and attitudes toward various facets of life. Through culture people form a comprehensive idea and sense about order in this life. Within this perspective, Christian calling derives benefits from cultural activities that involve an entire way of life shared by a people. In any case, the revelation of God needs constant communication in new situations, and this entails access to cultural opportunities, possibilities, and sensitivity, which provide mediatory roles for faith.[57] In certain respects, the whole future of humanity links up closely with what happens in the field of culture that always remains an ambiguous human construct, needing some constant discernment.[58] As the communal expression of the self-understanding of a people, culture defines how people live, relate, and act. It communicates and informs the internal and intentional horizon of human consciousness.

An anthropological sense of culture thus recognizes that all human societies have culture. All people can be said to be cultured. Culture defines and marks human life. All people have culture, but not all have the same particular patterns of culture.[59] Culture itself highlights differences among people since boundary maintenance marks cultural life itself.[60] Besides, cultural differences appear within the framework of a presumed common humanity in which judgments of truth, beauty, and goodness make sense.[61] But it must immediately be added that cultural identity builds upon, passes on, and carries forward earlier hybrid identities.[62]

Cultural identity means, in part, that people evaluate events differently and respond to different situations in unique ways. People experience and relate to similar events differently. They also take up and modify

---

55. Ibid., 31.

56. Ibid., 78.

57. Ibid., 40–41.

58. Ibid., 49.

59. Tanner, *Theories of Culture: A New Agenda for Theology*, 25–26.

60. Ibid., 36.

61. Ibid., 37.

62. Ibid., 57.

modes of expressions and communication according to personal autonomy, particular technical efficacy, a given characterization of situations, and some differentiated facets of life. While some people meet particular experiences with vigorous engagement, courage, patience, and enthusiasm, others encounter these same experiences with misunderstanding, laborious search, inaccurate assessments, and painful interventions. People construct their cultural identities within contexts of dialogue, interactive relations, and social interchange. In other words, our cultural identities orient us; they provide a frame for constructing meaning, distinguishing the trivial from the significant, and for understanding tastes, ideas, and aspirations. In promoting human agency within particular contexts, cultural identities always multi-laterally refer to a defining and evolving community.

Of course, cultural identity keeps developing and adapting itself to new historical circumstances. In this way, it continues to give meaning to people and provide models of action or mobilizing ideals. So, the notion of hybridity, which involves fuzziness, mixing, and mélange, unsettles any introverted gaze on culture, which would exclude any adjusting to and incorporating of new elements. The other side of cultural hybridity touches on cultural convergences and mutations so that crisscrossing and crossover constitute cultural beliefs in themselves.

In addition, differences among people have their origins in the ongoing life of people as maintained over generations by processes of imitation and example. People construct the character of their own living through group interactions and relationships. Cultural differences reflect distinct histories of particular groups of people.[63] The nonexclusive anthropological idea of culture highlights the basic and needed respect for different cultures and diversity of human experiences. Lives of individuals carry a certain primacy of social influence with them. Culture sets up and provides an original ambience and formative influence that society exercises on an individual primarily through unconscious means. So, apart from reflective choices and training, a person simply finds himself or herself exhibiting the linguistic skills, tastes, and thought patterns of the people among whom he or she has been brought up.[64] In other words, cultural construction, apprehension, and utilization of symbolic forms provide

63. Ibid., 4.
64. Ibid., 13–14.

patterns as well as social and psychological realities of life. They also shape persons and the way they tell stories about themselves, others, and the world.

Cultural forms come about as a result of local historical processes. Culture varies within social groups through specific patterns of behaviors that distinguish them. In this way, culture concentrates and expands attributes of social groups or societies. In this perspective, too, social habits and institutions, rituals and artifacts, categorical schemes and meanings, and beliefs and values mark the different ways of various peoples. A group or a society may have its own divisions, but these divisions do not alter the consensus character of the culture.[65] In fact, participants in contentious conversations within a culture rely on investment in common beliefs and sentiments. This basic reliance presupposes some widespread and shared understanding and the sense of what they disagree about with respect to details and particular significance. In the end, culture binds people together as a common ambience for engagement and action. In a culture, common attachment to and investment with cultural items of language, beliefs, symbols, norms, or practices hold its participants together.[66]

Complexity and diversity exist within any culture on the basis of complicated details of people's lives, which constitute as much the fulcrum of self-criticism as any other external out-group. Instead of culture simply being homogeneous, there exist internal contestations in every culture.[67] Debates within cultures arise from the intrinsic force of shared, even if contested, civic discourse and moral sensibilities that render humans worthy of regard and respect. In this way, culture continually rediscovers and presents itself as an agent of change. Within this framework, human beings steadily shape and recast what culture amounts to in any particular place and time in terms of its form and maintenance. Subsequently, no particular culture as a structure of signification can really claim inevitability.[68] The historical nature of culture ensures its dynamism. Culture shifts and moves as it absorbs and conflicts with new elements and meets new people and dynamics of relationships successfully or unsuccessfully. Human actors in a culture struggle over cultural elements precisely to

65. Ibid., 27.
66. Ibid., 57.
67. Ibid., 58.
68. Ibid., 28.

imbue them with some stable meaning and fixed interrelations that keep changing or reconfiguring.[69] This aspect of cultural dynamism results in competing and ongoing interpretations of the changing elements and perspectives within it in space and time.

Every culture attempts to offer an understanding of a genuine order of the world together with its celebrations, ambiguities, puzzles, and paradoxes. In other words, every culture provides ways of dealing and coping with human ambiguity. Culture also affirms and hence recognizes that life enjoys basic significance. Culture, then, means that this life cannot be a mirage. In fact, a certain fusion of the world as lived and the world as imagined takes place in every culture. This fusion also generates idiosyncratic senses of reality and purpose for persons. Through its symbolic forms, culture sums up and embodies answers to life that others have offered and appropriated over time and perhaps over generations. Various cultural trajectories and dynamism arise from convictions about reasonable, practical, humane, and moral living.

THE INTEGRATION OF CHRISTIAN FAITH AND CULTURE

The integration of Christian faith and culture, or the inculturation of the Christian faith, arises from their convergences as well as from their being intricately yet simultaneously woven into the fabric of people's lives. In order for effective inculturation to take place, words, deeds, and witness need to go together. The word of God needs to take root and bear fruit personally and concretely for individuals. As an act of witness, the practice of inculturation properly takes place in freedom, love, and dialogue.

The integration of faith and culture arises from the pastoral and ministerial demand of promoting, strengthening, and validating local churches. A local church integrates both the Christian faith and the local cultures. This integration also includes the incorporation of local personnel who consolidate the faith by ministering in effective ways to the Christian communities. After all, the Christian faith expresses itself within the cultural and spiritual life of daily interactions, worship, and catechesis as incarnated in the language and native habits of the people. A living faith has indigenous forms of religious life and spirituality inspired by local character, culture, history, actual contexts, and vision for the fu-

---

69. Ibid., 56.

ture. Of course, a healthy integration of faith and culture also implies a local identity open to the universality of the Church.

Besides, a living faith engages cultural forms and expressions of daily cooperation, mutual respect, and the human search for common and religious values that can transform society. Such a faith further identifies with the genuine aspirations of the local contexts, especially with the anxieties, sufferings, and problems of the poor, the marginalized, the oppressed, the voiceless, and the vulnerable. Living faith touches on and engages precisely the cultural norms, imaginations, and creative ways of living. In addition, there exists a cultural horizon to religion since culture censors allow for the symbolically and socially acceptable. In effect, religious faith cannot but be very much influenced by cultural evaluative responses. People live by images of life communicated to them by obtaining historical and cultural categories, expressions, and language.[70]

That is not all. Christian faith expresses personal relationship with Jesus and the experience of following him in discipleship. In this light, Jesus demands of his disciples that they do not exploit or oppress one another, but care for life, experience the joy of living, care for one another, and promote the common good. These demands of Jesus nourish and reassure the life of Christian faith. In spreading the Christian faith, it becomes imperative, then, to acknowledge the liberating divine authority with which Jesus acts, lives, and speaks. A Christian disciple holds fast to faith in Jesus's divine power by rooting the self in prayer and surrendering to Jesus and his vision of the kingdom. In a certain sense, Christian faith demands the renunciation of all savage ambition and competitiveness and the embrace of smallness and vulnerability by freely welcoming the least and the neediest in Jesus's name and image. The smallest acts of kindness and honesty get divine approbation. Also, Christian faith eschews all cliquishness. The disciple must share the blessings of life with all, particularly the disadvantaged, marginal, and outcast.

Moreover, mutual sharing and hospitality express mutual forgiveness, which Jesus's proclamation of divine forgiveness makes present. Besides, a close disciple of Jesus renounces his or her preoccupation with possessions, gives them to the poor, and follows the poor and indigent messiah. Christian faith renounces all ambition and desire for arrogance

---

70. Gallagher, *Clashing Symbols*, 4.

and coercive power.[71] In fact, Christian discipleship demands that people give priority to the reign of God and to its moral demands for service and care. In this light, the kingdom of God incorporates and consecrates one to a life of service of the community in Jesus's image.[72]

Christian faith enhances the willingness to live not only for this life but also for the life to come. The enhancement draws strength from purity of intention, the necessity of choosing between God and wealth, trusting in God's providential care, the reverence for sacred or holy things, rooting oneself in prayer, and living by the golden rule.[73] Rootedness in this world means that concrete, personal, public, and social consequences flow from the vision of the Christian faith. The needs and demands of the Christian faith signify that Christians recognize and change entrenched structures of sin continually. In this way, as faith embraces cultural realities, it also becomes able to purify the dehumanizing aspects within it.[74]

On the other hand, in involving the total process of human activities, efforts, and achievement, culture holds social heritage, which people receive and transmit. In this sense, culture gives form, rhythm, color, meanings, and symbols to social existence that maintains and advances life and makes possible human self-realization. As expressive of human purposes and efforts, culture imbues people with claims and interests, feelings and imaginations, and disparate expectations and visions. All these elements imply that the spread of faith always needs to involve elements and impulses of culture, however fragmentary and incomplete this involvement may be.[75]

In fact, in the process of integrating faith and culture, fidelity to Christ sometimes implies the rejection of some cultural elements not compatible with the liberative message and practices of Christian faith. For example, a cultural belief or practice that degrades women or sanctions the violations of women's rights would be contradictory to Christian ethos and exigencies. Oftentimes certain elements in a culture still cover up and diminish the humanity of some people in society. Conversely, there can also be some fundamental agreement between the Christian message and

---

71. Ibid.
72. Ibid., 120.
73. Ibid., 155.
74. Ibid., 107.
75. Niebur, *Christ and Culture*, 33.

some cultural elements or exigencies. There can be significant convergences in the hunger that culture and faith satisfy. In this light, for example, a cultural element of respect for persons would be compatible with the Christian message. As noted, Christian faith can also be seen as continuous as well as discontinuous with a given culture in certain respects. Where Christian faith and a given culture agree, Christ may, for example, be seen as fulfilling cultural aspirations. In a situation of crisis, people can also see Christ as the restorer of the institutions of a well-functioning and flourishing society. Or again, Christ could be seen as inviting people to attain a life of love, spontaneous goodness, and freedom beyond the law or norms.[76] Certain elements of Christian faith and practice could fit quite well with elements of a culture in a given context and time.

Nonetheless, we never fully achieve the process of integrating faith and culture, which always implies some selection and inclusion within a given set of social circumstances. In effect, it serves us well to see the polarity between Christian faith and culture as reflecting two horizons and sensibilities in tension so that justice and love, creation and redemption, wrath and mercy, and Christ and culture forever continue to intermingle or relate closely.[77] In this clash of loyalties, as it were, lies a certain battle for the hearts and imaginations of people. With a Christian lens, Christ always and readily transforms and converts nonliberative aspects of culture as he lifts them up to God.[78] After all, cultural realities themselves can carry much spiritual meaning.

TOOLS FOR CHRISTIAN INCULTURATION

The process of bringing faith and culture together means that Christianity and rational inquiry belong together, that a close relationship exists between a reasoned understanding of culture and faith. Christian faith can express itself intelligently and culturally. In this regard, inculturation must not become a matter of convenience, conjecture, and perhaps, biting anxiety. In taking root in order to bear fruit, faith needs to be open and sensitive to local situations. This also means, however, that the process of inculturation deals with actual lives of the people. It further implies that we discern the ways through which Christ may already be present and

76. Ibid., 42, 127.
77. Ibid., 159.
78. Ibid., 195.

active in a given culture. And inculturation succeeds when it offers some common grounds for conversations that come with recognizing and identifying similar interests on which people can compromise or agree.

Already existing values, sources of identity, and modes of behavior, as well as codes of conduct and ideals, provide the setting and broad context through which people consciously forge common grounds.[79] In this regard, we have desirable tools that can help us in listening well to a given culture in order to understand and make possible a transformation of faith by culture and vice versa. First, any approach to culture needs to be holistic. We need to always appraise any given culture as a whole.[80] When we fragment a given culture, we distort it and it becomes susceptible to misinterpretation and misrepresentation. Second, an illuminating approach to culture needs to address the question of where the forces that shape and influence a culture come from in terms of group boundaries and world senses. Furthermore, a helpful approach to culture pays attention to the issue of social change, not simply as a deviation from the mean but also as a vehicular context that brings improvement. Knowing the dissonances that mark the advent and progression of social change helps in appreciating the dynamics within a culture.[81]

It must also be stated clearly that in appreciating a given culture we instruct ourselves about the perspectives of the speakers and hearers as well as their inner and outer world senses.[82] Preserving the integrity of traditions, authentic voices, continued liveliness, and intelligibility of ways and views about life as well as the integrity of messages that offer meaning and signification help in describing and understanding a given culture. After all, we build much identity in human life and relationships by contrasts. Pluralism of perspectives within a given culture forms the baseline for intercommunication and shared memory, cohesion and continuity, and eventual linkages, renewal, and affirmation. These dynamics also provide for community living and the resources a community can count on from time to time.

Ways of evangelizing vary according to circumstances, time, and place. This fact demands that Christians adapt their message accordingly.

79. Schreiter, *Constructing Local Theologies*, 40.

80. Ibid., 43.

81. Ibid., 44–45.

82. Ibid., 57.

Irrespective of the approach adopted, however, evangelization entails witness to a fuller life since such experience provides the grounds for faith. Evangelization also entails a vitalizing proclamation since faith comes from what people hear and what people hear must be preached. Besides, the process of proclaiming the Christian message requires that Christians revisit local cultures through community processes, which call for sensitivity to the positive aspects of local traditions. Further, community processes imply openness, wide consultations, and active involvement of the locals in order to have an authentically local expression of the Christian faith. In fact, ordinary people can define very well the direction of the future on the basis of realistic assessment of their needs and the demands of their situations. Additionally, in our contemporary contexts, the use of the mass media cannot be ignored in spreading the gospel. The mass media can reach and pierce into the consciences of people. Moreover, the use of sacraments remains vital for the task of evangelization. This also means that faith finds its living expression in the concrete life of the believing community.

The foregoing considerations remain important because the advent of the Church in various African lands, for example, brought with it indiscriminate discouragement, rejection, diminishment, and sometimes outright destruction of African customs and cultural values interpreted as in complete contradiction to the will of God. In such circumstances, early evangelizers put forth little effort to understanding the religious wealth and response of local communities whose cultures and ways of being they then denigrated.

CONCLUSION

Leadership, guidance, correction, and encouragement form the staples that feed the integration of faith and culture in any given context of life. As implied throughout this chapter, the integration of faith and culture may involve some adaptation and accommodation, assimilation and indigenization,[83] acculturation[84] and enculturation,[85] and contextualiza-

83. Indigenization refers to changing things in order to fit local meaning and culture. It often involves adapting beliefs, customs, and practices to local ways.

84. Acculturation refers to the process by which an individual or a group modifies its culture as a result of contact and exchange with a different culture.

85. Enculturation refers to the process by which an individual learns and adapts to the accepted norms and values of the culture in which he or she lives through repetition.

tion.[86] The Christian faith always needs acceptance and openness to other cultures and traditions through some forms of liberative synthesis. It also needs some variety of translations of positive evaluation of cultures, especially indigenous ones. In other words, it behooves all committed Christians to continually enter the thicket of inculturation that always brings the Christian faith into the cultures of particular people.

Inculturation benefits the church as a whole and every individual Christian. In any case, the encounter between the church or the baptized person with a certain cultural context needs to result into a new transformation that honors the authentic Christian message as well as the best values and aspirations enshrined in a given cultural context. True and worthy processes and practices of inculturation imply an authentic blending of the Christian experience into the culture—that is, in the totality of a given life of the people so that Christian experience becomes enfleshed in it. In this way, inculturation animates, orients, and motivates the entire life of a people by giving it new unity and communion. The gospel needs to assume the best of human culture and sanctify it.[87]

Faith cannot be lived well on the fringes of the realities of life or arrangements of a given historical and inevitably cultural society. Faith needs to be involved with concrete and diverse questions, struggles, and hopes that every culture embodies in its center or periphery. In faith, we cannot ever give up on humanity. In other words, correlating faith with culture touches on respect for the dignity and diversity of cultures. As culture enlarges the breadth and terrain of faith, the revision of some established order through the liberty of the gospel and audacity of faith also takes place. In-depth conversion and renewal of culture belong to the very heart of the demand of faith that always aspires to a fuller life and to the great and forthright power of the resurrection.

As it were, the resurrection of Jesus provides the most potent pill against the final say of extrinsic validation and power on the significance

---

Enculturation establishes roles and functions and sets up a context of boundaries and correctness that governs the societal meaning of the acceptable and nonacceptable.

86. Contextualization refers to the process of adapting meanings and ideas, beliefs and values, and practices to fit the demands of particular settings of life. The process of contextualization implies that the authentic encounter with God takes place in time and space. This historical character of the encounter also means that the appropriation and consequences of the gospel happens within the narratives that arise from particular and shared experiences of the community.

87. Ruwaichi, "Inculturating the Gospel and Evangelizing Culture," 49–50.

of human life and hope in God. Within the Christian framework, the resurrection means the affirmation of Christ among us (i.e., in our midst). It refers to Christ who has become the force of liberty in our life and who we celebrate in our community. Of course, the real presence of the risen Jesus exists beyond sight and touch, but it always stimulates growth of human relationships, understanding, and reconciliation. In this way, the victory of God the Father, radiant in the liberating presence of the risen Jesus, happens here and now, within history, in our world.

The extraordinary reality of the presence of the risen Jesus in the ordinariness of life stimulates existence with enthusiasm and steadfast confidence. The real personal presence of the risen Jesus provides consolation, light, and hope beyond human support. To put it differently, the resurrection transforms the world as it furthers the flame of human availability, which transcends the barriers of time and space. Within a context of continuity and discontinuity, the real presence of the resurrected Christ inspires interpersonal liveliness amidst daily life that makes relations among people present, loving, and caring. The resurrection potential and newness reform human assessments and re-shape human practices and allegiances according to the priority of life over death.

At the same time, we must add that the resurrection demands the force and dynamics of active faith. In this regard, the next chapter discusses a biblical text of Isaiah 40:1–11 in order to highlight and give a picture of how active faith summons and inspires people toward an ever-fuller life.

Isaiah 40:1–11: A Case of Active Faith

Comfort, O comfort my people, says your God. Speak tenderly to Jerusalem, and cry to her that she has served her term, that her penalty is paid, that she has received from the LORD's hand double for all her sins. A voice cries out: "In the wilderness prepare the way of the LORD, make straight in the desert a highway for our God. Every valley shall be lifted up, and every mountain and hill be made low; the uneven ground shall become level, and the rough places a plain. Then the glory of the LORD shall be revealed, and all people shall see it together, for the mouth of the LORD has spoken." A voice says, "Cry out!" And I said, "What shall I cry?" All people are grass, their constancy is like the flower of the field. The grass withers, the flower fades, when the breath of the LORD blows upon it; surely the people are grass. The grass withers, the flower fades; but the word of our God will stand forever. Get you up to a high mountain, O Zion, herald of good tidings; lift up your voice with strength, O Jerusalem, herald of good tidings, lift it up, do not fear; say to the cities of Judah, "Here is your God!" See, the Lord GOD comes with might, and his arm rules for him; his reward is with him, and his recompense before him. He will feed his flock like a shepherd; he will gather the lambs in his arms, and carry them in his bosom, and gently lead the mother sheep. (Isa 40:1–11)

INTRODUCTION

THIS CHAPTER SEEKS TO identify the key issues pertaining to active faith that Isaiah 40:1-11 highlights as the symbol of a compelling power that can always transforms human societies. Active faith takes full measure of judgment and the lives of real people so that they act responsibly and take forward their existence. This chapter also intends to show that a close reading of the text offers a hermeneutic for understanding the experience of faith in God and human efforts in realizing the freedom that God truly symbolizes. Paradoxically, the herald for freedom that God's coming brings in Isaiah 40:1–11 seems to disagree with the conventional wisdom of everyday life. As people variously strive for a human fullness of life, a critical question that Isaiah 40:1–11 poses becomes, "Would extraordinary human efforts alone be enough for extraordinary liberation?" This chapter begins by looking at the background of the text. It then proceeds to articulate and analyze its chiastic structure, highlights the ramifications of the analyses, and ends with a conclusion. Without a doubt and within the guiding interests of this work, the building up of the human experience and expression of familyhood always requires the ingredient of active faith. At any rate, countless realities constantly enervate and gnaw away at individual, communal, and societal wellbeing. Besides, conditions of life change and new possibilities and alternatives of existence keep arising in this life.

BACKGROUND

In the standard account behind the text of Isaiah 40, Judah surrendered to Nebuchadnezzar in 597 BCE following the siege of Jerusalem, whereupon Nebuchadnezzar took King Jehoiachin and a number of important members of the society to Babylon. Unwisely, those left behind to control the affairs of Jerusalem rebelled against King Nebuchadnezzar, and this led to the destruction of Jerusalem in 587 or 586 BCE and the removal of a further group to Babylon.[1]

Isaiah 40–55 represents the prophecy of someone who lived during the Babylonian exile. The prophet addresses his message to a disillusioned people with weakened faith in God. The people left in Judah after 587 BCE became disillusioned since the deportation of their leaders led to the breakdown of public order, at least at first.[2] Jerusalem lay ruined and abandoned. The destruction of Jerusalem had ended the public official cult.[3] The message of Isaiah 40:1–11 directed itself primarily to the Israelites residing in Judah. No thought of any exiles existed. The people of Jerusalem and Judah would receive their reward and recompense in the

1. Coggins, "Do We Still Need Deutero-Isaiah?" 82.
2. Goulder, "Deutero-Isaiah," 352.
3. McKenzie, *Anchor Bible: Second Isaiah*, xxv.

divine shepherding to come (vv. 1, 11). The standard metaphor of *shepherd* stands for kings; God becomes a caring shepherd-king, attracting and carrying his people.[4] The proclamation of God's coming announced this good news for the cities of Judah, and this could hardly be done by exiles in Babylon. Isaiah conveyed his message at a time of weeping and not singing. In this light, the *wilderness* becomes doubly significant, both as an example of the barriers in human experiences that must all yield to the royal progress (v. 4) and as a reminder of the first Exodus by which the Israelites encountered God.

Behind the text of Isaiah 40:1–11 lies the notion of divine council of God as an incomparably powerful creator and redeemer. The opening words (vv. 1–2) transport the hearers, though without any description, into the heavenly council from where the prophet overhears the word spoken by God and the reiteration of the covenant promise.[5] In verse 1 someone with a nonspecific identity declares that God wants to console the people. The voice announces in verse 2 an appeal to the feelings, intelligence, and will of the hearers.[6] We have a picture of God seated on the throne, surrounded by heavenly beings who worship him. The divine council authorizes a prophetic call. This context that sets the prophetic call comes with great significance, for true prophets, as intermediaries between the people and God, can see and hear what happens in God's council. And the prophet as a representative of the people expresses the community's exhaustion and does so in traditional lament language.[7]

PRELIMINARY OBSERVATIONS OF THE TEXT

The text of Isaiah 40:1–11 employs the form of dialogue in which it becomes easy to distinguish the speakers. The speakers coincide with the prophet, God, and two unidentified voices. From the unidentified heavenly voices, variously characterized in commentaries as angels or messengers of God, the prophet receives his commission.[8]

In Isaiah 40:1–11 the presence and coming of the Lord dominate, and God speaks imperatives to bring comfort (vv. 1, 3, 10). The double pen-

---

4. Stuhmueller, "Deutero-Isaiah," 369.

5. Ackroyd, "The Book of Isaiah," 353.

6. Pelletier, "Isaiah," 985.

7. Clifford, "Isaiah 40–66," 574.

8. McKenzie, *Anchor Bible: Second Isaiah*, 17.

alty of verse 2 refers to the disaster of 587 BCE in which the Babylonians overturned the kingdom of Judah and left Jerusalem shattered and abandoned.[9] *My people* in verse 1 asserts God's covenant with a suffering people who were in pain and desolation. In this regard, reference to the cities of Judah symbolizes a people who were weak and needy and who suffered much neglect; God's coming promises concern, redemption, and care for them.[10] The imperatives of the verbs *comfort* in verse 1 and *lift up* in verse 9 emphasize the urgency of the message of *good tidings,* which verse 9 repeats twice. Good tidings proclaim and announce hope for a suffering people. Herein lies the élan of deliverance or expansive liberation. The initial voice in verse 1 refers to God's commanding comfort for his people; angelic speakers then bid hearers to make ready his way. A voice then orders the prophet to cry and make a proclamation of God's coming, but his replies strike a pessimistic note. The command to make his proclamation shocks the prophet. He says, "What shall I cry?" (v. 6).

The human condition lacks stability; it unveils itself as profoundly fragile. Intrigue, bad faith, and seditious tendencies frequently make the human condition fickle and treacherous. This understanding highlights the perspective of human sinfulness that marks this world. The voice in the text speaks of and sets human frailty and hopelessness in a theological language: "The grass withers, the flower fades, when the Breath of the Lord blows upon it; surely the people are grass" (v. 7) yet "the word of our God will stand forever" (v. 8). The mountains probably symbolize present difficulties that will be swept away (v. 4).

The prophetic message proclaims the visibility of the radiant glory of God on the highway because the mouth of God has said so (vv. 5, 8). The promise of God lasts; it does not fail. The word of God remains steadfast; it endures forever (v. 8). The word of God and the deed it achieves have an enduring reality. The event of God's word actuates liberating experiences for people. God's word and work constitute a single reality. In contrast to the word of God, we can liken human life to withering grass and fading flowers. As fragile and fraught with inconsistencies, human life always remains fleeting (v. 8). Human devices, ways, strategies, and measures often remain inadequate for the kind of comprehensive liberation that God's purposes and plans would effect.[11] In the context of verse 6, constancy

9. Ibid., 16.
10. Watts, *Word Biblical Commentary,* 90.
11. Ibid.

signifies fidelity to mutual obligations.[12] The contrast in verse 8 amplifies the skepticism about the integrity of human beings; people do not always preserve their loyalty for long.

The unreliable character of the transient measures and strategies of human beings need God, hence the proclamation, "Here is your God" (v. 9). God comes with power symbolized by his might and arm, which he uses on behalf of his people (vv. 1, 10). At the same time, God, like a shepherd, acts tenderly; he nurtures and patiently leads his straggling flock (vv. 2, 11).

The prophet's message cannot be anything but surprising. The temple existed no more; Jerusalem lay in ruins and was no longer a proud city; and the people had lost their liberty and organizational identity. Marked devastation, famine, death, and distress typified the ordinary lives of the people. Reduced to rubble, Jerusalem only boasted a few ragged and poor survivors: no king, no significant commerce, no political significance, and no active temple service or annual pilgrimages.[13] Years of exile had devastated all Judah. Yet to the heart and locus of this poignant experience (i.e., Jerusalem) the prophet directed the announcement that God would return to take up his place again. As a result, the speech of God controls the movement and spirit of the text. The divine world discloses itself as full of liberative impulses and imperatives that imply acts or aspects of liberation: comfort (v. 1); speak tenderly (v. 2); prepare the way of the Lord (v. 3); make straight (v. 3); cry out (v. 6); get up to a high mountain (v. 9); lift up your voice (v. 9); do not fear (v. 9); and say to the cities of Judah (v. 9). All these moving verbs focus on God as an active and liberating agent in shaping history. This God actuates hope, creative promotion, and joy.

The proclamation in the text does not, in fact, announce the return of the exiles from Babylon; rather, the proclamation declares the coming of the Lord. In point of fact, the text does not make evident an original rootedness in history. On the one hand, the very beginning of the section (40:2) poses a problem for a supposition of a Babylonian setting that leads someone to say, "Speak tenderly to Jerusalem." On the other hand, the prophetic speech cannot be made in Jerusalem readily and easily.[14]

---

12. McKenzie, *Anchor Study Bible: Second Isaiah,* 16.

13. Watts, *Word Biblical Commentary,* 79.

14. Goulder, "Deutero-Isaiah," 353.

Already from the preceding observations, we can recognize and appreciate that people often feel frail and hopeless when overwhelmed by economic, social, political, and military and vested interests of big bodies or organizations. Yet the thrust of Isaiah 40:1–11 points out that the word of God ultimately decides all; the word of God has the power to cause a withered and perishing people to blossom and flourish. Jerusalem and the cities of Judah, which symbolize people that circumstances marginalize and alienate from the tables of privilege, indeed become the bearers of good tidings. God directs his presence and calls to all the disenfranchised. The key issue with Isaiah 40:1–11 lies in the experience of exile characterized by uprootedness, alienation, and disorientation in which a people or a community participates.

THE CHIASTIC STRUCTURE OF THE TEXT

Isaiah 40:1–11 has an inbuilt interpretative chiastic structure that offers an insight into its main focus. The structure of the text may be presented thus:

A Comfort, O comfort my people, says your God.

B Speak tenderly to Jerusalem, and cry to her that she has served her term, that her penalty is paid, that she has received from the LORD's hand double for all her sins.

C A voice cries out: "In the wilderness prepare the way of the LORD, make straight in the desert a highway for our God.

D Every valley shall be lifted up, and every mountain and hill be made low; the uneven ground shall become level, and the rough places a plain.

E Then the glory of the LORD shall be revealed, and all people shall see it together, for the mouth of the LORD has spoken."

F A voice says, "Cry out!" And I said, "What shall I cry?" All people are grass, their constancy is like the flower of the field.

E' The grass withers, the flower fades, when the breath of the LORD blows upon it; surely the people are.

D' The grass withers, the flower fades; but the word of our God will stand forever.

C' Get you up to a high mountain, O Zion, herald of good tidings; lift up your voice with strength, O Jerusalem, herald of good tidings, lift it up, do not fear; say to the cities of Judah, "Here is your God!"

B' See, the Lord GOD comes with might, and his arm rules for him; his reward is with him, and his recompense before him.

A' He will feed his flock like a shepherd; he will gather the lambs in his arms, and carry them in his bosom, and gently lead the mother sheep. (Isa 40:1–11)

From the chiastic structure, we can make a number of observations from the interpretative parallelisms. The parallel AA' announces the promise of comforting care. The theme of consolation stands out. God cares for his own and for those who trust in and wait for him. Yet God comes according to his plan. BB' announces the promise of reward and makes an offer of reassurance. CC' voices and depicts the heralding of good tidings. DD' emphasizes the fragility of human nature. This parallelism confronts us with the inescapable character of the transience of human life. EE' speaks of God's glory and Breath as liberative vehicles that transform and redeem creation. F stands as the centerpiece of the chiasm. The chiastic structure of Isaiah 40:1–11 zeroes in on F (v. 6), which constitutes its central piece. This central piece, or the *inclusio*, laments the fragility of human capabilities and efforts.

Structurally, then, the whole text directs itself to the *inclusio*. In fact, the *inclusio* accentuates human weakness, notwithstanding the promise of triumph of life over death. Noticeably, a movement from doing away with a difficult and painful past to a future of promise marks the structure of the chiasm as well. But the passing past and the promised future exist in a real and dynamic present that remains beset by human weakness. Nonetheless, the real and dynamic present as the field in which liberative activities occur provides the basis for positive relations and human community. Or again, the presence and the coming of God gain a foothold in the dynamic and concrete present. In the present, God comes as a warrior and a shepherd who saves or redeems. The liberative experiences or events, actions or behaviors, understanding, and life of God can variously unburden and emancipate. God refreshes and enlivens the humanity of people, individually and communally.

PROPHETIC CALL AND FAITH

In the current text of Isaiah, the call about God's coming in fact goes out to a marginalized and oppressed people, namely the people of Jerusalem and cities of Judah (40:9). The prophetic call urges these people to prepare for and unveil God's glory in a new way for a renewal of creation. This message of radical and liberative propensities imbues Isaiah 40:1–11 with burst of joy and hope. So, God oddly and characteristically works in and through the experiences and cries of the burdened and those in bondage but who also take some initiative at self-announcement and in so doing, become partial agents in shaping histories. In this way, the human arena becomes the scene of God's liberative activities. In this sense, too, Israel stands for a people abused and victimized or embedded in human situations of oppressiveness and powerlessness but who have not given up the task and responsibility of working out others' and their own social emancipation. The working out of human emancipation does, indeed, manifest the eruption of God into personal and interpersonal drama.

Furthermore, Isaiah 40:1–11 depicts a transcendent and immanent God who also explodes the limits of human contingency and ideological or propositional circumscriptions. This understanding further implies that, in practice, God cannot be bracketed in by human interests and categories of the powerful and influential. The text in verse 5 says, "The glory of the Lord shall be revealed, and all people shall see it together," while in verse 8 it adds, "The word of our God will stand forever." In other words, the God of Isaiah 40:1–11 expresses himself as inherently the God of faith. This God can also be subject to human theological doubt. Verse 6 expresses this theological pessimism thus, "A voice says, 'Cry out!' And I said, 'What shall I cry?' All people are grass, their constancy is like the flower of the field."

The location of verse 6 as the *inclusio* of Isaiah 40:1–11 underscores the need for an active faith that goes beyond the goodwill of humans in truly realizing a prosperous future for the suffering. The pessimistic response of the prophet in verse 6 also needs to be understood in the light of the shattering disintegration of the people and the kingdom of Israel. The promise of survival simply shocks and awes the prophet. In the shock and awe lies the necessity of active faith in endowing human efforts with steely confidence, inspiration, and an enduring sense of significance. The revelation of God's liberating purpose always connects with the established frailty of human beings.[15] Active faith implies confidence in the presence and power of God, the recognition of the dependence of human beings on God, and an understanding that God's word and deed ultimately triumph over all. As forging a bond and an intimacy with life itself, faith connects with uprightness and effectiveness of God's word.[16] Here it becomes important to realize that where the word of God abides God also becomes present.

Where the work of God dwells, God's word resides. The utterance of God's word effects God's work. If we utter the word of God we effect God's presence; when we do God's work we make God's presence real and concrete. God's word as an efficacious power derives from divine resplendence and initiative that effect God's presence in the midst of humans and creation. The glorious and great God can be seen more gloriously and magnificently or become more radically perceived if burdened people make God present both in word and in their expansive and liberative actions. Accordingly, faith means that in this life the vocation of suffering human beings or of a burdened people consists in acting upon the word of God and responding to and living out the expansive demand for fullness of life in ways and terms that sanction harmonious and just relationships among people. Faith in God's unfailing word inspires the exigency for the full life. This exigency needs to constitute the source from which liberating human activities emanate and spring.

HUMAN AGENCY AND THE MIRACLE OF GOD IN HISTORY

It must then be set forth that active faith entails attunement to the message of salvation, deliverance, and assent to expansive truth that puts the focus of one's existence outside of oneself. In such faith, trust and loving self-communication become interwoven in ways that expand the horizons of actions and attitudes.[17] Furthermore, such faith offers the élan for self-commitment toward truly liberating enterprises that also deeply reverence the dignity of life and living ties among people, in spite of differences. Active faith reveals itself as transcendent in its presence and self-manifestation; its concrete efficacy, meaning, and purpose bring

---

15. Ackroyd, "The Book of Isaiah," 353.

16. Ibid., 354.

17. Dulles, *The Assurance of Things Hoped For*, 274–75.

salvation to people.[18] In this way, natural forces, military might, political power, wealth, or any other humanly created agencies do not become the placeholders of final trust.[19]

Therefore, verse 6 as the *inclusio* of Isaiah 40:1–11 focuses on the act of faith as a work and word event or affair in the enterprise of consoling and healing our problematic world. In spite of frailty, human beings can still be part of the moral miracle of God in history as long as people harness their desires, postures, and passion resourcefully in view of a steady focus on liberative fullness. In these ways, people truly participate in divine care that makes God present or manifest the good tidings, care, and comfort to which verses 1, 9, and 11 refer. Whatever attentiveness one can give to issues of brokenness that seek to crush the human spirit and alienate people from one another always helps in bringing about restorative and creative healing or wholeness to life. The human's sacred task and vocation consists in bringing healing and a sense of wholeness to a broken and hurting world. In other words, a way of life that cultivates radical friendship and bonding with life manifests an intimacy with life itself.

In the prophecy of Isaiah 40:1–11, the prophet speaks of the presence, existence, and common inheritance of the people (i.e., their faith in God). Yet there exist a lot of obstacles, symbolized by the valleys, uneven grounds, and mountains of 40:4. We need to recognize these in order that we may rise above them and in so doing, realize a future of promise. We do not have an easy route to bring about a future of real peace and hope. In effect, Isaiah 40:1–11 suggests a theophany in historical and cultural contexts of oppression and the felt experience of powerlessness. The highway of verse 3 for God's coming points to a world-encompassing theophany. Part of verse 5 asserts, "Then the glory of the Lord shall be revealed, and all people shall see it together." Even the representational proclamation in verse 9, "Here is your God," expresses a language of theophany, namely, God's advent. Besides, verse 9 conjures up the *religious emotions, hopes,* and *joys,* albeit associated with pre-exilic cultic and contextual celebrations when people sang the songs of Zion.[20]

---

18. Ibid., 176–277.

19. Ibid., 280.

20. Tidwell, "The Cultic Background of Isaiah 40:1–11," 48.

Further, Isaiah 40:5, 9 as constituting a glory theophany of God remain associated with the rule of God as king in 40:10–11.[21] God's advent reverses the misfortunes of people so that it occasions joyous celebration and singing (40:10). But the coming of God takes place through the desert—that is to say, through the resourceful overcoming of the experiences of captivity that people live. So the highway of God symbolizes the cultic location of the heart and human relations wherein God meets and encounters concrete men and women. Barriers of selfishness and naked greed, recklessness, and self-delusion beset this location. These obstacles must yield to the expansive life and freedom that God's coming (v. 11) and God's overwhelming presence usher in. The human heart and human relationships become efficacious through love that active faith brings.

In the text of Isaiah 40:1–11 we also deal with theological doubt and theological exile. Experiences of pain, suffering, and tragedy can cast doubt on the promise of a faithful and effective God. In the circumstances, the sense of good news (i.e., God's presence in the midst of all travails and tribulations) can easily be lost. The prophet acknowledges, "All people are grass, their constancy is like the flower of the field" (40:6). This acknowledgement implies that extraordinary human efforts for expansive liberation cannot simply be enough for an encompassing experience of success. Such efforts repeatedly require faith in order for them to sustain and realize the hope that inspires the impulses for the full life. The *inclusio* (v. 6) underscores the fact that people lack constancy; they lack steadfastness on account of their human fragility. Human steadfastness resembles grass and flowers. From a purely human point of view, the promise of comfort and care that embraces all people, which comes through human liberative efforts, seems hopeless. Yet people can always count on the promise and assurance of the effective word of God.

Not surprisingly, then, our inner steadiness and peace remain unpredictable. Precarious courage and harmony mark us. Our hope always remains pervious to subtleties of seasons, memories, and anxieties that come with history. We easily panic. Fears can darken our horizons and days and skew our thoughts and imaginations as they hang over us threateningly. At the same time, we all remain capable of new energies that readily focus us on and support our present efforts at better living. We can

21. Ibid., 49.

heal life's wounds through wisdom, openness, and light. We then do not give up on the humanity of others as well as our own.

The prophetic call in Isaiah 40:1–11 summons human efforts for expansive liberation as well as confidence in the presence and power of God amidst what may appear to be, humanly speaking, hopeless odds. Human dependence on God, particularly amidst much struggle, pain, dividedness, and separation, truly makes possible the preparation for God's sacred collaboration with men and women and his spiritual victory over the entire world. In all human liberative enterprises, God remains the one to whom people need to pay allegiance and remain pointed as they discern their particular steps or course of action or behaviors. The enduring and directing energies for transforming particular personal and social frameworks dwell, grow, and deepen in a context of active faith.

Therefore, Isaiah 40:1–11 has an insightful bearing on the matter of active faith and hope as people contend with domination and social upheavals. This is also to say that in everything God can work through willing human agents and bring about respectable, prosperous, and just living. Isaiah 40:1–11 indicates that we can always find the courage and faith to do right in the face of social human ambiguity. We can reach out beyond ourselves and act on behalf of others while at the same time placing our trust in God. In the face of precarious conditions and affliction of others, our favorable circumstances and influences always demand of us that we act on their behalf. In actual fact, much of social conflicts and sufferings (which Isa 40:1–11 assumes and entails) that destabilize and wreck societal wellbeing occur as a result of lack of human tolerance and cooperation.

CONCLUSION

When we strive to marshal human resources and efforts that aim to set right injustices or human conditions of living, we fail at steadfastness if we do not let God's word inform, energize, and motivate the enterprises from the beginning, middle, and end. In spite of the burden of human weakness, Isaiah 40:1–11 proclaims an ongoing realization of God's kingdom through the lowly and the poor. In this way, God boldly summons all people to a life of diligent work, just enterprises, and confident hope. God creates and redeems all. Isaiah 40:1–11 assures the sequence of events from suffering, humiliation, and abandonment to a new beginning, fulfillment, and joy.

In the text we have the itinerary from poignant fear and vulnerability to recovery of freedom and self-respect. We have a movement from victimization and the absence of justice to historical agency and unparalleled warmth and fecundity. The trajectory that characterizes Isaiah 40:1–11 demands faith as its motivating and inspiring vehicle in life. In the end, Isaiah 40:1–11 seems to underscore the understanding that extraordinary human efforts alone cannot bring about true expansive liberation. God can surprisingly achieve much through human frailty buttressed by the vigorous grip of faith. Activities prompted and inspired by active faith can spring surprises and shatter all ordinary expectations on which people base their routine actions or conventional paths people draw for themselves. In this way, people learn to execute the tasks that come with their calling within given contexts with humility, wisdom, and dedication to the common good.

In short, active faith sends us forward into new forms of resourceful human living. This sending forward demands that we offer our labor, sacrifice the urges of our egos, and offer our lives while deeply trusting God. In other words, the creation of the experience and expression of human familyhood cannot come about and thrive without the continual sustenance and fervor of active faith. Without active faith human efforts easily stagger at the edge of despair or hopelessness, or at least the risks remain real possibilities. But the flowering of active faith can particularly take place in a vital community called the Church, a theological portrait of which forms the subject matter of the next chapter.

3

A Portrait of a Vital Church

INTRODUCTION

THIS CHAPTER SEEKS TO identify the paschal mystery, conversion, apostolic succession, unity, and communion as key to understanding the vitality of the community called the Church. This chapter also discusses how these elements offer a framework for understanding the freedom of the Christian faith, which strives for human fullness. In other words, the vitality of the community called the Church depends on the founding and supportive experience of the paschal mystery, the goodwill that conversion brings, and faithfulness to the apostolic tradition, all with a focus on the unity and communion in the Church.

THE FOUNDING EXPERIENCE OF THE PASCHAL MYSTERY

In the first place, the paschal mystery refers to the life, death, and resurrection of Jesus Christ and the Pentecost or the mission of the divine Breath.[1] The paschal mystery reveals the lordship of Jesus (i.e., his divinity) because, in his resurrection, Jesus stands historically and eschatologically revealed as the breath-baptizer.[2] Or again, "The paschal mystery reveals Jesus' divinity because in the paschal mystery the risen Christ stands eschatologically revealed as the efficacious source of a divine reality, of the Breath of God Herself . . . the risen Christ stands . . . revealed . . . as God."[3] The revelation of Jesus's divinity in the paschal mystery puts the mortal ministry of Jesus in a new light and experience of confidence. This means also that Jesus embodied in his mortal ministry and in the paschal

1. Gelpi, *As We are One*, 109.
2. Ibid., 110.
3. Ibid., 75.

58

mystery God's saving intentions toward a sinful humanity with a unique incarnational normativity.[4] The paschal mystery reveals Jesus's religious vision as a human icon of the divine mind (i.e., as endowed with unique revelatory normativity).[5] In effect, then, "Christianity offers fragile, fallible, sinful humans the promise of a life-giving relationship with God through justifying faith . . . to the Church which results from the Incarnation and Pentecost."[6]

Although the incarnation grounds the paschal mystery, the incarnation and the paschal mystery constitute a single event in which God acted with immediacy and directness. The incarnation reveals that in the human event we call Jesus of Nazareth, we encounter the human experience of being a divine person. God's self-revelation in Jesus culminates in the paschal mystery.[7] Through the incarnation humanity encounters a divine person incarnate, a sinless embodiment of how God wants humanity to live and ultimately become.[8] The incarnation endows Christianity with an essentially historical character. The revelation of Jesus takes place in history, culture, and human experiences. And the Church derives its existence from the incarnation as the culmination of divine creative activity that brings into existence a new supernatural eschatological order. This order restores, recreates, inspires, and calls forth humanity to fullness.[9] Through the divine Breath God becomes our future; the future becomes the reality of God drawing near.[10] In fact, Christian faith concerns the future toward which we move yet grapple with sinful situations. From this standpoint, the paschal mystery reveals the ultimate destiny of Jesus's disciples, which is participation in his risen life with God in heaven through complete transformation in his Breath.[11]

Subsequently, through the paschal mystery the Church comes to know Jesus in the power of his Breath, which has an inherently practical character to it.[12] The paschal mystery manifests God's free and gratuitous

4. Ibid., 76.

5. Ibid., 83.

6. Ibid., 3.

7. Ibid., 75.

8. Ibid., 111.

9. Ibid., 108–9.

10. Ibid., 109.

11. Ibid., 94.

12. Ibid., 111.

intervention in history in order to undo the consequences of human sinfulness.[13] In light of the New Testament, this also means, however, that in the gospels we find the realities, values, and meaning of the Christ event. The themes, teachings, and allusions of the linkages in the gospel narratives dramatize the different ways of Christian participation in the risen life of Christ in the Breath. And the constantly abiding element in the gospel narratives coincides with Jesus's proclamation of divine reign, which has profound egalitarian social consequences.[14] Concretely, Jesus, in the gospel narratives, lays strict terms for humane, accountable, and responsive leadership in the community of his followers. Anyone in the community of Jesus's followers must never ape the oppressive ways of the kings of the Gentiles. Jesus denounced oppressive legalism and rigorism of the scribal class; instead he proclaimed forgiveness of sins.[15] In other words, Christian leaders should not lord it over others or use their leadership positions for personal aggrandizement, financial profit, or to exploit or abuse others. Authentic leadership consists in service that builds up the human community.[16] Jesus's proclamation stands in contrast with self-righteous legalism, religious rigorism and elitism, needless and burdensome multiplication of religious obligations, needless sanctification of human customs, hypocrisy, and violence of the heart.[17]

Jesus proclaimed God's kingdom, but he refused to pattern God's reign on the oppressive kingdoms of the world. He rejects any grounding of God's reign on law, coercion, and power politics. Instead he insists that genuine worship of the Father exists in mutual forgiveness and love of enemies, which authenticate worship.[18] In Jesus's vision of the Kingdom, mutual forgiveness tests the authenticity of prayer and provides a fundamental condition for membership. And love of enemies offers the ultimate test of mutual forgiveness.[19] The reign of God dwells in a place of radical inclusion; such a place also partakes of hope, richness in diversity, and marks itself by the absence of exploitation or silencing of others.

---

13. Ibid., 113.
14. Ibid., 118.
15. Ibid., 164.
16. Ibid., 82.
17. Ibid., 165.
18. Ibid., 118.
19. Ibid., 82.

As such, the reign of God positively justifies human differences and diversity. The reign of God, then, critiques the inner attitude of self-absorption that undermines liberative human relations. In other words, Jesus saw his community as the family of God. Christ left behind a vision of an ideal community and the gift of the Holy Spirit. This also rightly means that the spotlight needs to linger searchingly on how his followers give voice to those ignored in the corridors of power and how they exhibit faith that realizes simple dreams and insists on small miracles of life.

Furthermore, the reign of God symbolizes the kind of community Jesus calls into existence—namely, a community that identifies itself by a culture of discerning obedience, unconditioned trust, and all-consuming love.[20] This community roots itself in nonviolence and sharing. Or again, the community Jesus calls into existence determines and measures its commitment by the marks of obedience to the Father, radical, unconditioned trust, and the all-consuming and forgiving love of the Father.[21] Following Jesus stands the conventional society on its head; it means being free to share materially with others on the basis of needs.

JUSTIFYING FAITH AND CONVERSION

Concretely, Christian faith and life begin when people convert—that is, when they become attracted by and committed to the excellence incarnated by Jesus affectively, imaginatively, and rationally.[22] This commitment to Jesus, which coincides with the offer of justifying faith, creates the novel context or frame of reference that engages the whole person in understanding and appreciating engaging realities of life. In this regard, justifying faith sets right the consciences of people so that they can live according to the norms and ideals of revelation in Jesus Christ.

> The vision of the kingdom functions as an ideal which both lures the consciences of believers at the same time that it stands in judgment upon the Christian community's failure to practice fully what it knows itself called by God to preach and embody in the name of the risen Christ and in the power of His Breath.[23]

---

20. Ibid., 81.

21. Ibid., 124–25, 201.

22. Ibid., 84–85, 157.

23. Ibid., 126.

From this perspective, spirituality becomes an organized way of relating to the Spirit of God vivaciously. All Christian life in the Church roots itself in justifying faith so that every genuine gift in the Church has its own validity. In consequence, all the gifts of the community need to be recognized, embraced, and fostered.

Justifying faith corresponds to the initial dynamic of the total process of Christian conversion, which has affective and moral dimensions. The first dynamic of Christian conversion, which mediates between affective and moral conversion by putting them in anew kind of relationship, grounds the experience and ongoing justification by faith.[24] Justifying faith coincides with faith in Jesus as God incarnate. It underlies the maturity of conversion. Justifying faith engages the total person to Jesus as God incarnate. Justifying faith "begins in repentance and culminates in the decision to let the divine Breath teach and empower one to live in the image of God's incarnate Son."[25] In this regard, Christian faith terminates in the person of Jesus Christ.

At the same time, it needs to be acknowledged and recognized that the Breath of the risen Christ effects conversion of individual Christians as well as the shared faith consciousness in communities through the outpouring of charisms. And shared consciousness in Christian communities comes about through shared memories and hopes, coordination of charisms, and collaboration of the members for a common future. Sharing of charisms entails, for example, the recognition of the prophets and evangelists who call the community to greater conversion and bring the gifts of prayer and healing that endow and infuse the Christian community with a vivid sense of God's efficacious presence.[26] The process of ongoing conversion bears fruit in charismatic ministries in the Christian community where one may serve as a teacher, healer, as one who prays, discerns, or leads.[27] When believers share charisms, they effect further ongoing conversion.

Or again, we need to understand that the Christian community, from its beginnings, forged a common identity by a process of ongoing self-interpretation of shared lives and communal awareness. Moreover, the

24. Ibid., 102.
25. Ibid., 97.
26. Ibid., 96.
27. Ibid., 97.

forging of common identity involves some agreement and understanding of the ultimate and proximate future to which the community feels called. Besides, shared awareness takes place through the mobilizing of gifts of the members in order to realize some of the proximate goals to which the community feels itself summoned. In order to sustain its witness, the Christian community constantly self-interprets itself in the light of grace, hope, faith, love, and a Christian passion for a just social order.[28]

Conversion thus requires that Christians look to the Breath to teach them how to live as children of God (i.e., how to submit to the demands of life in God's just reign).[29] And as already pointed out, initial conversion takes the form of justifying faith, which initiates repentance and culminates in the decision to let the divine Breath teach and empower one to live in the image of God's incarnate Son. And to live in Jesus's image requires faith in him and in God's Kingdom to transform this life.[30]

In fact, human existence demands a conversion experience. Fascinatingly, human beings continually subject themselves to evaluations so that they recognize and become aware of decisions and tendencies that inhibit them from positive and sound living.[31] In human conversion (which always involves a turning from and a turning to), a human being turns from irresponsible to responsible behavior in some realm of experience.[32] As a matter of fact:

> Responsibility means accountability to oneself, to others and ultimately to God. Conversion requires responsibility to oneself, because every convert through conversion comes to acknowledge that certain persons, ideals, principles, realities make legitimate claims upon one and measure the subsequent authenticity of one's choices.[33]

What is more, conversion requires accountability to others because it always occurs in a context of social arrangements and relationships; it also

---

28. Ibid., 112.
29. Ibid., 97.
30. Ibid., 96.
31. Ibid., 28.
32. Ibid., 69.
33. Ibid.

has consequences not only for oneself but also for other people affected by one's judgments and choices.[34]

When it comes to affective conversion we may note that hope forms its normative terminus. Affective conversion leads to emotional balance and health, imaginative flexibility and creativity, zest for life, and sensitivity to genuine excellence.[35] In affective conversion a person takes responsibility for his or her psychic health and intuitive response to the realities of life. Admittedly, a serious disorder in one's affectivity introduces disorder into the very judgments that shape human consciences; this disorder breeds moral malice and religious hypocrisy.[36] Besides, "[d]isorder disrupts the shared life of the community and therefore disturbs the peace which ought to characterize shared Christian living."[37] Communally, "the orderly exercise of the gifts exhibits due respect for an authority which serves the community's common good."[38] In fact, affective conversion infuses other forms of conversion with enthusiasm, emotional vision, flexibility, and imagination.

Conversion also takes place at the intellectual level, which has a significant bearing on the quality of one's beliefs and on what a person says. Living life on the basis of true beliefs enables one to form convictions and establish relationships on the basis of genuine intuitions and understanding. Intellectual conversion involves taking responsibility for beliefs by appealing to the norms of truth and falsity in measuring specific beliefs. This conversion also invokes norms of adequacy and inadequacy, which measures the frames of reference in which one fixes one's beliefs. In addition, intellectual conversion invokes the norms of validity, which measures the logical authenticity of deductive and inductive inferential thinking.[39] In the process, we develop concern for consistency between thought and what experience offers. Intellectual conversion belongs to the second dynamic of Christian conversion. Here it may be noted that the second dynamic of Christian conversion—its transvaluation of the other

---

34. Ibid.
35. Ibid., 102.
36. Ibid., 100.
37. Ibid., 147.
38. Ibid., 148.
39. Ibid., 74.

forms of conversion—grounds the experience of sanctification, which authenticates charismatic ministry of service.[40]

What is more, conversion also bears a moral aspect. Moral conversion enables a person to lead life by examples guided by authentic values that make possible a worthwhile life, self-respect, and self-love by means of which people can become open about others' and their own failures and weaknesses. Further, at the moral level, human conversion can be personal or public. Personal moral conversion draws attention to and judges interpersonal morality in terms of rights and duties while public moral conversion leads to the consciousness of the common good and social institutions that allow people to share in the goods of the community in a reasonable way.[41] Moral conversion, hence, enables one to take responsibility for one's motives as well as for the consequences of one's judgments and choices.

In further speaking about conversion, we may add that the religiously converted person responds to some historical self-revelation and self-communication of God in terms that revelation demands.[42] Such a person responds in faith. And for Christians this means that God revealed himself eschatologically and normatively in the incarnation of the second person of the Trinity and in the Pentecostal mission of the Breath.[43] Eschatological events reveal and conceal divine, transcendent reality, and such events often involve the saving collaboration between the creature and creator in an ongoing struggle of undoing the consequences of human sinfulness.[44]

In other words, Christians convert religiously when they confront in faith the divine reality revealed in the person of Jesus Christ. The incarnation, Jesus's ministry, the passion, the resurrection, and the mission of the Breath as events of Christian revelation judge the truth and falsity, the adequacy or inadequacy of a theory, or presuppositions about the reality of God. For the Christian, the Christ event remains paradigmatic of all human reality. Jesus's vision of the kingdom makes normative claims on

---

40. Ibid., 102.
41. Ibid.
42. Ibid., 69.
43. Ibid., 75.
44. Ibid., 113.

the corporate and personal consciences of Christian communities.[45] The events of Christian revelation also make moral demands.[46]

The ethical demands of Christian discipleship derive from Jesus's proclamation of God's reign and from the paschal mystery.[47] Jesus summoned his disciples to a religion of ideals. Jesus required of his disciples trust in the Father's providential care.[48] One who trusts in God's care for one's needs does not, for example, cling to physical supports of life as the decisive reality for which one lives. Instead such a trust means that one labors so as not to burden others and to have something to share with the poor and disenfranchised in a spirit of hospitality.[49] For Jesus the sharing of physical support of life ought also to break down all the conventional barriers among the people that sin erects in human society.[50] In this regard, the materially well off have the Christian responsibility to support the poor who cannot effectively decide for themselves.

In enhancing the process of genuine discipleship, a conversion experience illuminates life and impresses a new orientation and proper outlook on human life and the fabric of personal relationships. It creates a leaven of hope and freedom in human relationships that particularly pays special attention to the needy and the poor. The experience offers us an invitation to choose and define our basic attitudes with honesty, fidelity, altruism, and goodness. As a consequence, we reflexively begin to choose love over selfishness, justice over dishonesty, and compassion over malice. Furthermore, conversion alters our fundamental decisions with regard to the logic of life, which becomes one of sharing and solidarity that enhances and serves the common good. The frame of such logic of life contrasts with the selfish quest for profit as the ultimate criterion of all activities. Within the magnificence of conversion, we realize and share personal talents, abilities, and riches in ways that strengthen our bonds of life and friendships. At the heart of the experience and expression of conversion we find the spirit of authentic generosity. To some extent, we become a leaven that vivifies the lives of others.

---

45. Ibid., 121.
46. Ibid., 76.
47. Ibid., 80.
48. Ibid., 116.
49. Ibid., 81.
50. Ibid., 82.

APOSTOLIC SUCCESSION, CHARISMS,
AND CHURCH LEADERSHIP

The paschal mystery as a founding event and experience of Christian faith has been handed on through the witness of the apostles. The encounter of the apostles with the risen Christ gave them special authority in the Christian community. After all, their proclamation of the risen Jesus in the power of his Breath transformed the renewal movement in Palestinian Judaism, which Jesus formed into a church.[51] "After the resurrection, the disciples called Jesus 'Lord'... and in so doing they proclaimed Him the human embodiment of God. That proclamation created the shared faith of the Church."[52] The personal encounter with the risen Jesus effected a conversion experience in the apostles that they passed on. This also meant:

> The Church can know Jesus as its Lord and can finally understand the full saving and religious significance of His mortal ministry only in the power of His Breath . . . The apostles bequeathed to the Church . . . a kind of religious experience, an experience of religious conversion wrought by the empowering enlightenment of the Breath of the risen Christ . . . The apostles testified to their own experience of converted enlightenment and inculcated it in others.[53]

This is also to say, "The charismatic transformation of the disciples created their shared faith awareness as a community, taught them to embody corporately the mind of Christ through the sharing of the charisms in mutual ministry, and so created the Church."[54] The "revelation event that founded the Christian community was not constituted solely by the life, death, resurrection, and ascension of Jesus but also by the experience of that divine self-gift by Jesus' disciples."[55] When we speak this way we touch on the issue of apostolic tradition or succession. In regard to tradition, in the first place, we may note:

> The experience of the group that founds a society precedes its formulation of the fundamental law of the society. But after the

51. Ibid., 18.
52. Ibid., 111.
53. Ibid.
54. Ibid., 113.
55. Schneiders, *Revelatory Text,* 76.

formulation and commitment of writing of this fundamental law
... the society and its experience become subject to the foundational vision and experience as preserved in the written document
of foundation.[56]

Effectively:

> Tradition is the actualization in the present, in and through lan-
> guage, of the most valued and critically important aspects of the
> community's experience, or, more precisely, of the community's
> experience itself as it has been selectively appropriated and de-
> liberately transmitted. Tradition is the primary form and norm of
> effective historical consciousness, which is the medium of ongoing
> community experience.[57]

With reference to the Church, tradition needs to be understood, then, in
the following terms:

> Tradition, as the *foundational gift* out of which the Church's ex-
> perience unfolds throughout history, is the Holy Spirit who is
> the presence of the risen Jesus making the Church the Body of
> Christ. Tradition, as *content*, is the sum total of the appropriated
> and transmitted Christian experience, out of which Christians
> throughout history select the material for renewed syntheses of
> the faith. Tradition refers also to the mode by which that content
> is made available to successive generations of believers, the way
> in which the traditioning of the faith is carried on throughout
> history.[58]

Accordingly, "The importance of apostolic tradition arises from the
fact that it happened and because of the nature of what happened ... its
importance lies in its foundational and mediational character ..."[59] No
one of the generation that followed the apostles could give eyewitness
testimony to the life, death, and resurrection of Jesus that the twelve could
give; no one could claim to have received his commission directly from
the risen Lord as they and Paul had received. The apostles could share
with no one their mission, for that mission had to be given by the risen

---

56. Ibid., 66.
57. Ibid., 71.
58. Ibid., 72.
59. Ibid., 76.

Lord himself.[60] In other words, "When the early Church committed the apostolic witness to writing and recognized some of that writing as adequate to (though not exhaustive of) that witness, it created documents that would function, for all future time, as normative of tradition."[61] With respect to the Church, it must also be clear that:

> Tradition is handed on in a wide variety of ways differing in adequacy and importance, but the most important, indeed indispensable, mode is the celebration of the Christian community of the liturgy within which the Gospel is appropriately and truly preached.[62]

This means also that the transmission of the Christian tradition engages a variety of spiritualities that shape the faith life of Christians in the feasts and customs of popular religiosity and in the ongoing endeavors of theologians to discern the critical correlation between the symbols of the faith and contemporary culture. It also involves the ever-increasing literature of faith in catechetical instruction and sacramental preparation within the Christian family life. It further takes place through active involvement in and reception of the Church's ministry. Indeed, whenever and however the faith remains alive, tradition comes into expression, affected for good or ill, and is handed on.[63] In the end, apostolic succession refers to the whole Church itself rooted in the proclamation of the gospel; it also requires and presupposes faith.

With regard to apostolic succession, thus, we may note that it expresses the permanence and hence the continuity of Christ's own mission in which the Church participates. And under the particular historical circumstances of the growing Church in the early centuries, the succession of bishops became one of the ways, together with the transmission of the gospel and the life of the community, in which apostolic tradition expressed itself.[64] Also, "the evidence suggests that up to the end of the New Testament period leadership and other ministry were provided in each local Church by a group of 'elders' or 'overseers,' with no one person in charge except when the apostle or one of his coworkers was actually

---

60. Sullivan, *From Apostles to Bishops*, 40.

61. Ibid., 77.

62. Ibid., 80.

63. Ibid., 79.

64. Ibid., 8.

present."[65] The apostles could not do everything that needed to be done; they had to share their ministry.[66] The ministry the apostles shared with others during their lifetime had to be handed on for the church to continue and grow to maturity.[67] Subsequently, "*I Clement* does affirm that the founding apostles had appointed the first generation of local church leaders and had laid down the rule that when those men died, others should be appointed to succeed them."[68]

Evidently, then, the apostles shared their mandate with their missionary coworkers and the leaders in the local churches so that when they died apostolic ministry continued.[69] Over time, however, the "Christian faithful recognized the bishops as the successors to the apostles in teaching authority. The reception of the bishops' teaching as normative for faith is analogous to the reception of certain writings as normative for faith."[70] In the final analysis, "Christ founded the Church . . . he continues to guide it through the abiding gift of the Holy Spirit and . . . the Holy Spirit maintains the Church in the true faith."[71] This also means that "If one believes . . . that the Holy Spirit maintains the Church in the true faith, one must also believe that the Holy Spirit guided the Church in its discernment of the books that would constitute written norms for its faith."[72] Or again, "We have just as good reason for believing that the Spirit guided the church in recognizing its bishops as successors of the apostles and authoritative teachers of the faith as we have for believing that the Spirit guided it in discerning the books that comprise the New Testament."[73] Hence, in Christian self-understanding the Holy Spirit given by the risen Christ guides the church in such a way that allows basic structural development to be seen as embodying the will of Jesus Christ for his Church.[74]

In the context of the Catholic Church the fact of apostolic succession relates to Church governance, which involves due recognition of papal

65. Ibid., 14.
66. Ibid., 42.
67. Ibid., 53.
68. Ibid., 15.
69. Ibid., 223.
70. Ibid., 225.
71. Ibid., 224.
72. Ibid., 229.
73. Ibid., 230.
74. Ibid.

primacy as well as the acknowledgment that each bishop remains in his Church, understood as organic community, as a vicar and ambassador of Christ. That is also to say that the college of bishops, led by the bishop of Rome, forms the governing body of the Catholic Church. In other words, every proper sense of episcopal authority also has need of the development of appropriate structures of collegial governance.

What is more, the notion and approach of episcopal collegiality involves the consultations of bishops with one another, consultations between the pope and several representative bishops of the world, and consultations of the bishops in the Roman curia. In this way, the pope becomes better placed to act with the prudent counsels of bishops who have to live with his decision. Collegiality, then, can enhance the unity of the Church.

UNITY AND COMMUNION IN THE CHURCH

The unity of the Church, as reflected in the charity and harmony of the Eucharistic fellowship, reflects the unity of God and the bond between Christ and the Father.[75] In this regard, too, there cannot be a church unless there exists a worshipping community, but worship in itself without an accompanying spirituality cannot hold all people together.[76] Besides, the unity of the Church repeatedly requires the exercise of authority in the Church, which pleads and guides, exhorts and inspires, and persuades and motivates. Good quality authority inspires continued listening and conversations at various levels of cross-cultural dialogue and ethics, which motivates people to bear one another's concerns and cares so that they also become bound to one another. The exercise of such authority helps to resolve issues early and grasps the feelings of people on issues that they regard as of particular concern to them.

Of course, the empowering of Peter and the other apostles serves as the basis of the authority of individual bishops in their local churches.[77] At the same time, it must be added that the apostles shared their authority and responsibility of feeding the flock in common accord.[78] Besides, mutual love of the bishops glued and bound together the universal Church

---

75. Burns, *Cyprian the Bishop*, 151.

76. Brown, *Churches the Apostles Left Behind*, 98.

77. Burns, *Cyprian the Bishop*, 157.

78. Ibid.

over time.[79] In other words, the authority of the bishops, the unity of the episcopate, and the unity of the Church community hang together.[80] As leaders in the community, the bishop and presbyters or Church ministers act in the name of the community as a whole and to serve its interests rather than their own.[81] That remains their fundamental vocation. What is more, since authority in the Church exists for the purpose of proclaiming the gospel, service, and transforming people's lives, its exercise also calls for constant discernment. This also implies that authority in the Christian community needs a strong ritual of constructive dialogue, continual conversations, reconciliation, and recommitment that can assuage inflammation of passions among people. A good Church leader continually reminds and exhorts the community to repentance and united prayer.[82]

Furthermore, the ministry of leadership in the Church needs to stimulate, coordinate, and bring together the different ministries present in the midst of the people of God. Church authority truly requires multiplicity of charisms, functions, and ministries, always based on service, which relate with and enhance mutual understanding, communication, and dialogue among believers. Liberative Church life enhances the cohesion, peace, and communion of the community and the benefits of its Eucharistic fellowship. This fellowship further implies that the Christian community needs to have the right to choose, advise, and in extreme circumstances, depose its leaders.[83] In all exercise of authority in the Church, however, it remains the case that "Jesus alone is the model shepherd . . . What is characteristic and distinctive of his shepherding is not the authority or power he claims over the sheep, but his intimate knowledge of them and love of them."[84] Decidedly, then, discipleship has preeminence over offices and charisms or other distinctions.[85] In the light of Christian vocation, the Christian identity needs to always transcend any identity gained from the functions and exercise of authority.[86]

79. Ibid.

80. Ibid., 159.

81. Ibid., 15.

82. Ibid., 134.

83. Ibid., 49.

84. Brown, *Churches the Apostles Left Behind*, 93.

85. Ibid., 94.

86. Ibid., 100.

Membership in the Church also means that if Christ could give himself to the Church, so should his followers. In other words, if we love the Church in a personal relationship, the Church begins to symbolize a cause that truly attracts our generosity and self-giving love and service.[87] Paradoxically enough, that the Holy Spirit guides the Church does not mean that faults, sins, and stupidities in the Church should be masked. Oppression, venality, and dishonesty harm the inner vitality of the Church.[88] These acts need to be exposed, spoken against, and addressed properly, though always with love. In other words, seriousness about peace, reconciliation, healing, and forgiveness preclude killing each other, acts of malice, or an orchestration of vindication that destroys the good reputation of others. Such acts only leave the Church with a great deal of trepidation and foreboding and risks of mischaracterization of situations. Issues of accountability, participation, and resolution of conflicts require inclusive approaches that deepen the cohesion and attractiveness of the community called Church which does not also become obsessed with fears of all sorts. So belief in Jesus necessarily entails an ongoing commitment to live in a manner worthy of the belief.[89]

That is not all. In order for Christianity to face new situations meaningfully, it must have an element of the contemporary and of the original. The medium for this mediation entails a re-interpretation of the paschal mystery in the light of new situations and the new data of experience. The Holy Spirit preserves the past without corruption because the Spirit receives everything from Jesus and gives no new revelation.[90] In effect, rendering current the paschal mystery implies Christian commitment to freedom and truth, which come with openness to listen, learn, and serve present needs and aspirations. Bustling participation of as many people as possible through the use of participatory empowerment and practices of consultation and encouraging initiatives in the life of the Church enable friendly, neighborly, and collaborative Christian witness. As the Church strives to fully live out her call of being in communion, the Church becomes, in this struggling and ambivalent world, a true sign of hope that incarnates the self-giving life.

87. Ibid., 55.
88. Ibid., 56.
89. Ibid., 112.
90. Ibid., 108.

Additionally, the Church, at least insofar as its composition remains of sinful men and women, constantly needs to be open to improving and purifying its religious life, practices, and interests. While in this world, then, the Church will, from time to time, betray trust and confidence on account of personal and communal mentalities, backgrounds, and limitations. Shortcomings will attend the life of the Church in spite of all measures to realize greater freedom, discipline, and creative aliveness. Moreover, necessary criticisms need to be restrained and committed. Such forms of criticism need to inspire patience and constructive actions, which spring from co-responsible and renewal points of view. In short, sin, grace, and salvation, as words, may be old stuff, but as facts they lie at the heart of the fulfilling destiny of every Christian and every man and woman.[91] Indeed, "the very community of grace without which no Christian finds the true path to salvation itself desperately needs saving. Christians belong to an *ecclesia semper reformada*, a Church forever in need of reform."[92] It is not without reason that we call the Church one, catholic, and apostolic; but the living Church also remains fragmented, sinful, chauvinistic, and somewhat deracinated from its best apostolic tradition.[93] What is more, "the Breath of the risen Jesus continues to transform the institutional Church into a community of healing, life and grace . . . One must even learn to love the Church because of its sinfulness . . . sinfulness only manifests how desperately a sinful community needs the . . . atoning, forgiving love of Christ."[94] The Church repeatedly wanders through horizons of sin and error. Hence, the Church constantly needs new orientations and refreshing moments of new life.

CONCLUSION

The vitality, mission, and identity of the Church embody the ascendancy of hope in a world in which the temptations of defeatism and despair can be quite real. In setting the tone for liberative communion and fullness as its normative end, the Church not only gives meaning and direction to life, but it also proclaims the transcendence of human connectedness, which coextends with trans-personal and trans-social harmony. In this

91. Marcel, *Problematic Man*, 197.
92. Gelpi, *As We are One*, 4.
93. Ibid.
94. Ibid., 9–10.

proclamation, too, the exercise of authority in the Church establishes itself charismatically. In fact, every true gift in the Church brings with it some authority. People also grow in the authority of their gifts, yet in all cases "the authentic exercise of any charism ought to sanctify the one who exercises it and those to whom that person ministers."[95] Irrespective of forms and expressions, Christian life repeatedly needs more understanding in terms of service than of power or control and personal advantage in order that it preserves and fosters its own appeal and efficacy. When the community called Church inspires, motivates, and ignites passion and willingness for the gospel, people become truly involved in being Church. And for this to continue and expand, we need conversion. In this regard, we may immediately note that conversion constitutes the prophetic heartbeat of Church as family, something with which the next chapter deals.

95. Ibid., 99.

4

Conversion as the Prophetic Heartbeat
of the Church as Family

INTRODUCTION

THE PREVIOUS CHAPTER EXAMINED and inquired into the theological portrayal of a vital Church in this world. Against this backdrop, this chapter seeks to address the effectiveness, relevance, and significance of the metaphor of the Church as family in order to foster the mission of the Church as a community of disciples. At any rate, the Church as family communicates one authoritative way of understanding the Church that captures some salient features of being a community of grace structured as a human society. The metaphor of the Church as family implies living together in sharing, solidarity, mutual love, and support. It also implies right relational placement of persons in a context of dialogue and conversations as instruments of family communion. Understanding the Church as a community of disciples underscores the understanding that the Church bears the primary responsibility of spreading the good news of the gospel, of healing, and of uniting the human community.

In discussing and examining the metaphor of the Church as family, the chapter begins by reflecting on the theological rationale for and explanation of the metaphor. When the new energy and new life that the centering process of conversion brings forth emerge as key realities within the Church, she comes to truly exemplify and embody the family of God. Conversion activates and promotes continual evaluation, praxis, and rethinking of positive living. In so doing, conversion becomes a vital experience in the Christian struggle with the perspective and question of authentic humanity as it unfolds in history. Evidently, then, only through conversion can Christians truly establish the act and practice of receivable and acceptable freedom and the liberty of their existence in this world. In its approach, thus, the chapter highlights the theological justifications for the metaphor of the Church as family before addressing the question of discipleship and conversion as necessary in the self-understanding of the Church as family.

RATIONALE FOR THE CHURCH AS FAMILY

In the context of Christian faith, people can increase their awareness of common fatherhood and motherhood as sprung from God, the common brotherhood and sisterhood they share in Jesus Christ, and the common love that they have in the Holy Spirit. The Church traces her origin from the mission of the Son sent by the Father and the mission that the Holy Spirit perpetuates in the Church. The Holy Spirit enables and motivates the continued life and existence of the Church.

That the Church comes from God and goes to God establishes a profound sense of mission for the Church (i.e., as sent by God to proclaim the kingdom of God). This fact of being sent marks the Church with interior movements that construct and unveil her sense of meaning and purpose in the world. Such movements include gratitude, awe, respect, peacefulness, fulfillment, and joy. As the creative and generative power of fuller life, God floods the Church with the consciousness of total being, which unifies and transforms existence. The Church's divine origin, then, imbues her with an immense sense of responsibility for her mission with humility, being, and truth. That the Church originates from God further awakens and frames different levels of depth in her self-definition, vision, and imagination according to time and geography. The divine origin of the Church forms the stand from which the Church charts her life in terms of identity, expectations, direction, and location in existence.

In light of the preceding considerations, we see that, in one sense, the Church incarnates, reflects, and manifests the family of the triune God. As the family of God, the Church publicizes and extends visibly the mystery of the Trinity in time; the Church heralds the kingdom of God. In other words, she lives up to her true identity and mission if she marks herself by the dynamic elements of human convergence, union, and common search for God. Accordingly, the Church, under the impulses of the Holy Spirit, exists out of mission and for mission in proclaiming the good news. She enlivens and sanitizes humanity with the recognition and experience of transforming peace and the joy of the gospel, which reach out to various levels of human life, relations, customs, values, and world senses.

In her mission, then, the Church seeks to appreciate and transform the world with the liberative light that springs from the encounter with Jesus Christ. The Church bears witness to her mission by proclaiming saving truth and freedom, by means of service that favors human promotion and by making Christ present through authentic Christian life. Indeed, the Church can only carry out her mission effectively in the light of her own self-understanding. The Church as the family of God depicts a viable model for realizing the mission of the Church, which includes dialogue, cooperation, and contextualization of the good news.

In fact, the metaphor of the Church as family asserts fraternity, communion, and fellowship among people. In this way, it confirms the basic claims of humanity in which joys and sorrows blend together in individual and shared existence. When the metaphor of the Church as family fosters the emergence of living ties among people, it energizes and enlightens the human imagination with the immeasurable forces of love, union, and hope in Christ. The sense of connections and closeness that comes with the Church as family readily breeds benevolence and hospitality. It also nourishes honesty and fidelity, exchanges and care, and mutual sharing and constant dialoging that make people real brothers and sisters to one another. Thus, the metaphor of the Church as family deepens the human awareness that people can always be brought to relate and live together. The interweaving image of the Church as family underscores the values of communion and solidarity. The experience of human togetherness readily provides people with a sacred sense of meaning. Further, it builds and expands fraternity in Christ (i.e., the consciousness of becoming brothers and sisters of the same quality). In Christ, all become adopted sons and daughters of God. In other words, the spirit of fraternity lies at the heart of the Christian message, for human fraternity consists in nothing other than charity itself. And it must be noted that charity implies pooling together with others, communicating, and generously sharing fruits of experience, work, and faith. In the mutuality and reciprocity of charity people put their full person, their full existence, alongside of others and give more fully of themselves and their resources to others whom they regard as brothers and sisters of the same quality.

The metaphor of the Church as family also means that the Church fundamentally consists of a communion of baptized men and women. It corresponds to a community of free and responsible engagement of all children of God together with their diverse charisms. In fact, the metaphor of the Church as family invites and challenges us to recognize that we cannot believe the good news of Jesus unless we have a change in mind and heart that brings us together. In other words, to live as disciples of Jesus, as members of his Church, demands of us a profound experience of conversion—that is, a change of mind and heart—so that we see and treat all as brothers and sisters of the same quality. In conversion, we commit daily to communion and peace, forgiveness and reconciliation, understanding and compassion, courage and perseverance, and love and truth, *and not* to divisions, dividedness, or violence. Day by day, the journey of conversion brings a new way of life rooted in an inner empowerment and peace that enable persons to become reconcilers and peacemakers. After all, to live as a Christian, to live as an authentic disciple of Jesus, implies being at peace with oneself, often in spite of many trials and sufferings, and at peace with others, because one lives by the peace of the risen Christ.

Theologically, the Church as family as an experience and expression of Christian discipleship finds justification in the Trinity, in the incarnation, in Vatican Council II, and in the first African Synod.

THEOLOGICAL JUSTIFICATIONS OF THE CHURCH AS FAMILY

Trinitarian Basis for the Church as Family

The Church corresponds to and develops a community of disciples of Jesus Christ with a heart and relevance to the lives of people. She does so by adapting to prevailing circumstances and sustaining people's confidence in life. She urges fraternity in Christ. She forges and molds a community of brothers and sisters of the same quality in Christ. When we speak this way we allude to an understanding of the Church in terms that make apt the metaphor of the family. The Church as family originally points to the Holy Trinity as the basis and source of the Church. Within this perspective, the Church can truly be seen as a sacrament of the union and love of the Father, Son, and Holy Spirit. Within the Trinity exists a constant experience of steady coming and self-giving. This integrating and harmonizing experience generates the movement from the Father to the Son, the returning, glorifying movement from the Son to the Father, and the unifying, bonding movement between both of them of the Holy Spirit. The salvific movements within the Trinity generate and create us so that we can return and glorify God and become united and bonded among ourselves.[1] Unencumbered by physical limitations of time and space, the divine persons enjoy the capacity to offer themselves to one another with such a totality and fullness of love that they share not a similarity but an identity of divine life.[2]

No breakdown of communication exists among the divine persons since they do not labor under the limitations of space and time or the social limitations of embodied persons. Divine persons share the same identical mind, the same identical will, and the same identical life. The divine persons dwell lovingly in one another and nurture one another in ecstatic and life-giving ways. Fullness of presence and mutual self-gifts in the divine experience enjoy inherently communal and social character. In this regard, the risen Christ confronts us as Lord, as one who bears the Father's divine name and who shares the Father's very life. And we also know the risen Christ as a life-giving Spirit.[3] Subsequently, the triune God can only stand historically self-revealed as a social reality—that is, as the supreme exemplification of interpersonal social relationships and communion. The free self-communication of the triune God in history, in revealing the social life of the Trinity, simultaneously discloses to human beings a new way of relating to one another as persons who can transcend anything left to their own resources.[4]

Accordingly, through faith we experience the unity of the divine persons as an upper limit that human persons, relationships, and societies can approach but never fully attain. The explanation lies in the fact that lives of the divine persons blend with vital fullness unavailable to physically embodied persons. The interpersonal, social relationships of the divine persons enjoy supremacy, totality, and perfection. The communal and social character of the divine experience makes it symbolic and therefore, historically revealable. We can legitimately imagine the triune God as a divine family and therefore progressive union with God

---

1. Fraile, *God Within Us*, 15–16.
2. Gelpi, *Committed Worship*, 165–66.
3. Ibid., 166.
4. Ibid., 178.

as incorporation into the divine family.[5] The divine reality can thus be understood as an analogy with human experience. In other words, divine communion, community, and society exhibit an analogy with fullness of human social experience.

We can also legitimately imagine adult conversion as familial and progressive socialization into God's human family in this world, the Church. Incorporation in the human family of God unites the Christian believer to the triune God. Admission into the Church symbolizes the beginning of a graced assimilation into the divine family itself. The historical revelation of the divine family endows graced social relationships with a sacramental character.[6]

Christological Basis for the Church as Family

The Church as the family of God also points to the Christological character of the Church. In his salvific mission, Jesus chose to be born into a human family. As a result, the family assumed a unique value and embodied a continuation of Christ's saving mission. The symbol of the family thus emerges as a privileged instrument of salvation.[7] Through the incarnation Jesus takes our humanity, becomes our brother, and now lives in solidarity with believers as his brothers and sisters. Jesus takes on humanity in order to communicate divinity. In the incarnation, God and the human being become one so that the incarnation itself becomes a process of union between the divine and human that heals, elevates (divinizes), and redeems humankind. Through the incarnation Christ becomes a member of the human family; he takes on human flesh so that he understands himself as a member of the human family. Incarnation as a communication of divine love and solidarity between human beings means that the Church also becomes a vehicle for promoting communication and solidarity among people.

All baptized Christians form a fellowship of men and women with God and with one another in Christ. Baptized Christians form a community of brothers and sisters of the same quality in Christ. In fact, the first Christians tended to think of themselves as belonging to the family of God. This tendency traces itself to Jesus's *Abba* experience. Jesus

---

5. Ibid., 173.

6. Ibid., 167, 178.

7. Ruwaichi, "The Newness and Pastoral Implications of the Church as Family," 25.

experienced God as a constant origin of his very being; he experienced and expressed an intimate and privileged kinship with the Father. Jesus immersed himself in God; he felt a unique intimacy with the Father, as the Father dwelt in his very being. At a profound level of being, Jesus experienced himself and lived in depths where God lives. This level of depth equipped him with the energies of spirit and truth, respect and adoration, union and love, forgiveness and compassion, peace and silence, and prayer and humility. God made his home in Jesus, and Jesus made his home in God.

Jesus invited his disciples to share in the intimacy of his experience with God. Drawing on his own sense of relating to God as Son, he tried to teach his followers to live in his own image as God's sons and daughters seeing, feeling, and living the experience of oneness with one another (Matt 25:40; John 15:15). Jesus stressed the need for his disciples to love one another (John 15:12–13). Jesus invited his disciples to commit themselves to universal love (Luke 10:29–37). By his own example he wanted his disciples to include all people in the solidarity of His Father's love and family (John 17:21).

As the first Christians thought of themselves as belonging to the family of God they lived with a genuine sense of human kinship among themselves. In this way, they lived the concrete experience and expression of faith in the Risen Christ. Notably, because Christians normally called one another "brother" and "sister," the pagans suspected them of living in incest. In speaking of the early Christian community, Acts 2:42–47, for example, captures this lived experience in the following way:

> They devoted themselves to the apostles' teaching and fellowship, to the breaking of bread and the prayers. Awe came upon everyone, because many wonders and signs were being done by the apostles. All who believed were together and had all things in common; they would sell their possessions and goods and distribute the proceeds to all, as any had need. Day by day, as they spent much time together in the temple, they broke bread at home and ate their food with glad and generous hearts, praising God and having the goodwill of all the people. And day by day the Lord added to their number those who were being saved.

The Church as Family in Vatican Council II

Vatican Council II's way of speaking of the Church expresses a consistency with an ecclesiology of familyhood. Vatican II clarified that understanding the Church takes shape around the notions of the presence and activity of the Holy Spirit, who brings the faithful into communion with God, whether in the form of Father, Son, or Holy Spirit. The Holy Spirit gives each member of the community the gifts considered necessary for building up the Church. In effect, through baptism and confirmation, all Christians share in the apostolate of the Lord himself.[8] Perfect equality of all members of the Church prevails; all relate as equals. Common rebirth of Christians in Christ gives them a common dignity, common grace as sons and daughters with the same quality, and a common vocation to expansive freedom and love. They all enjoy true equality with regard to the dignity and activities common to all the faithful in building up the body of Christ.[9] Here one should note that the ordained, in fact, do not have complete or all the responsibility for the Church.[10] In a word, our way of relating within the Church needs to resemble that of a well-ordered family, with the added proviso that the majority of the faithful have reached adulthood. So, adult-to-adult relationships largely constitute being the Church.

Vatican II employed categories that helped stimulate theological reflection of the nature, life, and functioning of the Church. In these categories the Council speaks of the Church as the people of God and as Holy Communion, metaphors that implicitly and eloquently hint at the synthetic spirit of familyhood. In these metaphors, belonging to the Church empowers and commissions members of God's family to reach out to one another generously and lovingly. The salvation wrought by Christ applies and directs itself to all. The call of Christians, as members in Christ's family, effectively entails spreading bonds of harmony and unity among people through noble qualities and aspirations.

Vatican II invites Christians to build up the Church of communion in which members possess full equality but a variety of roles and functions. Every Christian bears a responsibility for a wondrous life and marvelous

---

8. *Lumen Gentium*, 33. All the documents of the counsel in this chapter are taken from *The Documents of Vatican II: All Sixteen Official Texts Promulgated by the Ecumenical Council*.

9. Ibid., 32.

10. Ibid., 30.

mission of Christ in the community in virtue of the natural and supernatural gifts received from the Spirit and the gifts acquired through culture, study, formation, and experience. Members of Christian communities and their pastors enjoy equal dignity but exercise different ministries and functions according to the gifts they have received. Without doubt, they all share responsibility for the life and mission of the Church.[11]

True to the spirit of familyhood, Vatican II acknowledged and recognized the Church as a sign and instrument of communion with God and of the unity of the whole human race.[12] The vocation of the Church as a whole consists in proclaiming the good news of the love of God to every people and nation and indeed, to the ends of the earth. Wherever they live, Christians enjoy the same mission to all the people of their neighborhood, village, town, city, countryside, parish, and diocese. The bonds that unite men and women as sons and daughters of one Father, redeemed by Christ, and gifted by the Holy Spirit, wax stronger than any conventional barriers that separate them. The call of people, as children of God, consists in living together in love and harmony. Christian cultivation of unity in diversity witnesses to Christ and the triune God. The experience and expression of familyhood thus lies at the heart of the identity and mission of the Church. Indeed, the ordinary challenge of peace demands the reasonable equality of all, and the survival of humanity together raises the issue of death and life.

The Church as family means that God calls Christians into the dialogue that he already holds with all people through creation, their religions, cultural exigencies, their consciences, kinship ties among people, and the urge for peace that lies deep in every human being. This calling invites an attitude of openness to all and a readiness to offer friendship, listening ears, respectful collaboration, consultation, encouragement, and the sharing of religious experience.[13] In other words, whenever a Christian community discerns and acknowledges the liberative signs of the kingdom of God in cultures, in other religious traditions, and in secular movements, the community enables people to know that they belong to one another and all together belong to God. When the Christian community enables people to see and live their hidden unity, it gives the concrete world a

11. McGarry, "Church as Family: Sign and Instrument of the Unity of the Whole Human Race," 29.

12. *Lumen Gentium*, #1.

13. *Gaudium et Spes*, #22.

new horizon and peace in Christ. As an instrument of unity, the Christian community also becomes a sacrament of reconciliation.

Notably, tensions and differences mark common life, but how we deal with hidden fears and insecurities of relationships matters the most. And when reconciliation takes center stage in life, people can achieve a new framework through which they continually reconstruct new ways of life based on life-giving values. In other words, reconciliation means that people can always give birth to new life where it has faltered. As experience demonstrates, people can endure vilification and intimidation and emerge victors when they properly mobilize inward and outward resources of healing broken relationships. Reconciliation warms relationships and makes it possible for communities and individuals to re-establish, build up, and achieve expansive unity among people.

As a form of consciousness that restores goodwill, reconciliation often follows an appraisal of contention. It acknowledges functional diversity. Through it people listen to different perspectives in order to chart a new path for future coexistence. Conversations and storytelling mediate reconciliation because in the absence of inter-human communication, inward fixations accentuate conflicts in external relations. Of course, we cannot discharge the noble responsibilities of reconciling people through the practice of using untruths and of resorting to deceit and dishonest means to attain specified goals. From an existential perspective, thus, we can always face difficulties and reversals in this life honestly, carefully, and patiently. We can always ask and discuss questions frankly. We can always address challenges candidly and resourcefully.

The Church as Family in the First African Synod

According to the African Synod of 1994 in Rome, the community of believers constitutes the family of God alive with hope. Christian believers belong to the Father's family. They derive from the Son their fraternal embrace, which overcomes hate. The Holy Spirit molds believers into the image of the blessed Trinity.[14] The Church-family[15] has its origin in the blessed Trinity at the depths of which the Holy Spirit activates and en-

14. Message of the Synod, #3. The documents pertaining to the African synod in this chapter, particularly the "Message of the Synod" and "Propositions," are taken from a publication by Africa Faith and Justice Network, *African Synod: Documents, Reflections, Perspectives*, 72–86.

15. This is a variant of Church as family in various discussions or conversations.

courages the bond of communion. The Church knows that the intrinsic value of a community lies in the quality of relations that make it possible.[16] The good news proclaims the Church as family of God in this world. The same Spirit gives life to all.[17] According to the African Synod, the image of the Church as family emphasizes care for the other, solidarity, warmth of relations, acceptance, dialogue, and trust. It also signifies how authority needs to be exercised as service in love. Moreover, baptism initiates a person into the family of God. In fact, the interior momentum and logic of baptism call for conversion, which overcomes all particularisms and excessive ethno-centrism. Baptism allows the faithful to live with differences, in reconciliation, and in true communion as brothers and sisters of the same quality.[18]

The Father took the initiative to create Adam with a view to the Church as family. Christ, the new Adam and heir to the nations, founded the Church as a family by the gift of his body and blood. The Church-as-family manifests to the world the Spirit that the Son sent from the Father to create communion among all. Envy, jealousy, and the deceit of the devil can always tempt and drive the human family to racism, ethnic exclusivism, and both hidden and overt violence of all forms. These acts, in their turn, lead to war; to the division of the human race into first, second, third, and fourth worlds; to placing more value on wealth than on the life of a brother or sister; and to the provocation of interminable conflicts and wars for the express goal of gaining and maintaining power or for self-enrichment through the destruction or death of a brother or sister.[19]

What is more, the Church lives effectively as a family inasmuch as all Christian families become authentic domestic churches. The call within each family consists of fathers, mothers, and children living in the image of the Holy Family in the richness of love, which animates the heart of God. The Church-as-family further requires the creation of basic ecclesial and human communities as loci of inclusive fraternity and disinterested yet passionate service, solidarity, and common goals. The Church-as-family enables the Church to understand itself as communion, namely as

16. Message of the Synod, #20.

17. Ibid., #25.

18. Propositons, #8.

19. Ibid.

the people of God in which every member has both rights and duties and enjoys full respect and involvement in what goes on in the Church.

When we encourage the participation of each and every baptized person we help to identify issues that promote humane Church life through consultation and common deliberation. Implementation of common and consultative decisions needs to define the very nature of every authentic Church life. The involvement of people (which further requires concrete plans, strategies, money, and personnel) breeds and expands their sense of love, concern, and co-responsibility. In other words, the Church-as-family seeks to serve the entire human community. As a basis of unity and solidarity, the Church-as-family further implies sharing roles, involving as many people as possible, and emphasizing small communities and ordinary positive relations. Authentic Church life offers a context in which members feel their equality guaranteed, the sharing of responsibility recognized, and clear option for the disadvantaged members made. Or again, genuine Christian life provides mechanisms for transforming, resolving, and transcending all simmering and deadly tensions.

THE FAMILY AS THE NEXUS OF CENTRIPETAL
AND CENTRIFUGAL RELATIONSHIPS

In the family we reveal our presence, sense of generosity, and care as well as desires that connect us with others. What is more, a growing family does not simply present itself as a milieu of convenience and appeal, cheap entertainment, and comfort. More importantly, it presents itself as a place of growth in attitudes and dispositions of openness and honesty in living life. In this way, it forms our consciences and gifts us with a sense of involvement and a deep longing for an efficient presence as a source of security, energy, and hope.

Unquestionably, too, it would be naïve to assume that the family climate remains always rosy. Differences and misunderstandings punctuate family dynamics. While a vibrant family intensifies deep joys and unions that precede and follow feelings, its members can become deeply jealous and possessive of one another. The affairs of the family can be filled with struggles and failings. As a result, there can be much love and hate, tender care and greed, kindness and envy, offense and reconciliation, and cruelty and forgiveness within the family. Happily, when we feel union and harmony within the family environment, the experience generates a deep sense of freedom and worthiness.

As members of the same family, we tend to have strong feelings toward one another, by means of which we also reveal our functional identities and basic attitudes. In the process, we grow to live with familial spontaneity and with an outward thrust of the human spirit. In this sense, the family veritably discloses itself as a nexus of relationships: inward kinship ties of family loyalty and outward relationships beyond the family circles. Constant negotiations of these relationships and loyalties frequently shape every human being's growth. The family unit establishes or rather constitutes the basic condition for all genuine human development. Of course, the dynamics and expressions of the family vary according to place and roles of individuals. These dynamics depend, in part, on how individuals negotiate the sense of personal integrity within the context of a group (neighborhood, town, city, tribe, nation, race, sex). In fact, family relationships can assume corporate and territorial expressions because of family members, family location, family interests, and family influence. Additionally, the family survives and thrives on the continual remembering and narratives about the ancestors who lived before and from which the members inherit traditions that give coherence to their common life together.

In the context of the Church as family, we give further significance to the community, which locates people in space and time and within which individuals achieve full personhood. In this respect, individual freedom and worth and the community form pillars among which Christians' ethos and attitudes locate themselves. The promotion of the individuality, gifts, and talents of the members needs to coexist with the love and the responsibility to build up the body of the Church. This is also to say that we can only work out our personal salvation within the context of the community of believers. In the Church, individual and common destiny cannot exist apart from each other. A deep fellowship exists between these two species of the human destiny that shapes people's experience of the ecclesial mystery. In effect, part of the task of the Church as family consists in renewing and restoring the basic equality of all so that all can participate in the joy of living resourcefully. In this way, the metaphor of the Church as family challenges the Church to a calling and work of reconstruction of the human community.

On the one hand, violent ripping of the family fabric, for instance, constitutes an antitype of familyhood. On the other hand, in a context of a healthy family experience, members normally build each other up, have strong bonds of solidarity, and compassionately care for one another. Furthermore, as family members learn from common hardships of life, the experiences modify their approaches to existence and in so doing, enable them to develop attitudes and strengths capable of negotiating or triumphing over adversity of all kinds.

A deep conviction within the community of the Church as God's family relates to God's parenthood that makes us all brothers and sisters of the same quality. This also means that patriarchy, paternalism, authoritarianism, nepotism, and all forms of unfair discrimination must not have any respectable place in the Church as family. Or again, intolerance, bigotry, racism, tribalism, separations, and segregation contradict ties of spiritual kinship among Christian believers. Conversely, care for others, solidarity, acceptance, dialogue, and trust remain consistent with the nature and exigencies of the Church as family. Unity of purpose and shared commitments encourage the establishment of a Christian spiritual family. In this regard, the Church as family extends beyond the basic household as it orients itself toward the wider society. Accordingly, the locus of the Church as family expresses vital and organic connections with the wider historical and cultural contexts that continually nourish it with new questions, trajectories, and exigencies.

At the same time, members of the Church as family must learn how to handle well glamorous external influences since another's meat can become one's poison. Frequently, though, contexts and circumstances do indicate and distinguish appropriate from inappropriate influences and approaches that require due care and discernment. In any case, the gospel values need to always renew, strengthen, permeate, and guide the experience and expression of the Church as family. These gospel values normally include the beatitudes, reconciliation, collaboration, and sharing of resources, especially with people at the margins of society. When the Church as family functions satisfactorily, it often also means that conversion forms its prophetic heartbeat.

CONVERSION AND THE FAITH OF THE CHURCH AS FAMILY

Evidently, Christians embody and represent a people of faith, love, and hope called into the experience and expression of communion by the Trinitarian God to whom they wend their pilgrim ways. The Church as family bears a responsibility for the Christian faithful who live the call and challenge to embrace the healing entailed in conversion and integral reconciliation with oneself, one's neighbor, and God. This Christian demand concerns the individual person as well as the entire community. Conversion and reconciliation further imply that the Christian faithful live the call to cherish and strive after the typically Christian values. Thus, they need to yearn for the true, the just, the pure, the lovely, the gracious, the honorable, and the holy (Phil 4:8).

The Christian community truly becomes a family of God through conversion, sanctification, and sharing the gifts of the Holy Spirit. Conversion involves more than the question of sin. It deeply implies a renewed relationship with God and God's ways of acting. Sanctification signifies a day-by-day transformation that incrementally makes us more truly human. In speaking of conversion one may note, for example, that personal conversion establishes social accountability in interpersonal dealings with others. Socio-political conversion makes a person institutionally accountable to society at large.[20] Conversion and sanctification unite believers by teaching them to put on the image and mind of Christ. All this means that as they grow in faith and mutual charismatic service, Christians learn to treat one another as brothers and sisters of the same quality in the Lord Jesus Christ. As such, Christian life imitates the faithful obedience of God's incarnate Son. Sharing the gifts of service cements the bonds that unite Christian believers into a single family.[21]

CONVERSION: MEANING AND VARIETY

As noted earlier, conversion exemplifies an experience that grounds and authenticates the whole of Christian faith and practice.[22] In fact, conversion, which also means turning around, leads to an encounter with liberative experience that coincides with awareness of the divine or God as the source of spirit and light. The experience empowers people joyfully and

20. Gelpi, *Committed Worship*, 20.

21. Ibid., 158–59.

22. Ibid., 5.

courageously with freedom and life. Also, conversion takes place within a context of cultural presuppositions and imagination. In fact, it results from the action of God's grace, which heals, sanctifies, and elevates the natural powers of operation of the converts by creating within them the capacity to act supernaturally.[23] Of course, people come to grace through the mediation of the Church.[24] At the same time, an ever-deepening commitment to God can only be effected through ongoing conversion.[25] And ongoing conversion provides an indispensable precondition for authentic Christian worship. Further, conversion mediates the forgiveness of sins. In this way, conversion gives a convert victory over sin and death.[26]

As a movement, conversion enables people to account for the motives and consequences of their decisions to someone or to some community of persons. Conversion effects multiple changes in the life of a convert. In this regard, moral conversion turns the will of a person from a life of sin to the pursuit of moral goodness. Moral conversion teaches the affectively converted Christian prudential realism in the living of life.

Irrespective of how and where it begins, particular conversion transvalues into other forms. Affective conversion leads a person from an irresponsible resistance to facing one's disordered affectivity to the responsible cultivation of balanced, aesthetically sensitive emotional life that informs natural conscience. Affective conversion requires confrontation with the dark side of the personality—that is, with the snarl of both conscious and unconscious negative feelings like rage, shame, fear, and guilt, which prevent the free flow of the sympathetic emotions of affection and love.[27] A person who has cultivated affective sensitivity can learn to balance felt judgments with rational ones and vice versa. Here we may

23. Ibid., 9.

24. Ibid., 10.

25. Ibid., 6–7. Here it becomes important to note that integral experience of conversion involves an initial religious experience and encounter and ongoing conversion. Initial conversion is essentially a religious transformation, which entails turning away from unbelief to belief, from sin toward a life of sinless grace, and from exclusion from full sacramental communion with the community of disciples of Jesus to full communion with them. Initial conversion then brings with it moral, ecclesial, and social consequences. The notion of ongoing conversion refers to the lifelong process of openness of the converts that takes place in secular contexts and that touches on values, actions, and tendencies.

26. Ibid., 10.

27. Ibid., 74.

note the fact that affective conversion, which entails reason and receptivity to goodness, animates all the other forms of conversion. Furthermore, intellectual conversion leads a person from an irresponsible acquiescence in accepted beliefs to a commitment to validating one's personal beliefs within adequate frames of reference and in ongoing dialogue with others. Sociopolitical conversion leads a person from unreflective acceptance of the institutional violations of human rights to a commitment to collaborate with others in the reform of unjust social, economic, and political structures.[28]

Indeed, conversion makes a person responsible so that he or she lives in dialogue with those affected by his or her own judgments and choices. Personal conversion, in this sense, creates social accountability in interpersonal dealings with others. A person accounts for the motives and consequences of his or her behavior and conduct as he or she also becomes willing to shape his or her conduct in ongoing dialogue with others. Sociopolitical conversion, on the other hand, makes a person accountable to society at large. Responsible behavior recognizes the social, dialogic character of the human conscience.[29]

Religious Christian conversion, which mediates affective and moral conversion, turns a person from ignorance and indifference to the God revealed in Jesus Christ and through the action of the Holy Spirit to a life of faith. Hence, confessional conversion incorporates a convert into the one true Church.[30] In this light, Christian conversion begins in the heart. It demands that a convert renounce sinful attitudes that separate him or her from God.[31] In Christian conversion a person finds the will of God normatively revealed in the person of Jesus and in his vision of the kingdom. This conversion introduces the convert to the social character of the Godhead and the fullness of human redemption. Christian conversion calls for the re-evaluation in faith of every natural experience in the light of divine revelation.[32] In addition to suffusing Christian moral striving with zest for gospel living, Christian conversion also demands that the judgment of conscience that moral conversion sanctions submit not only

28. Ibid., 17.
29. Ibid., 20.
30. Ibid., 9, 17.
31. Ibid., 41.
32. Ibid., 29.

to naturally prudential judgments but also in prayerful discernment of the will of God that the incarnate Word proclaimed. In fact, Jesus's moral vision constrains the disciples' consciences as they stand in judgment over action that sinfully contradicts God's will.

Adult Christian conversion begins with repentance—that is, in a confrontation with the disordered passions and attitudes that prevent one from consenting wholeheartedly and without reserve to God. In repentance, the disordered heart confronts an incarnate God. A repentant heart touched by the Spirit of Jesus perceives the divine beauty incarnate in him and in people whose lives resemble his. That beauty and its simultaneous reality of truth and goodness lure the heart spontaneously with the promise of healing and of new freedom in God. The perception and grasp of this beauty take place intuitively and inferentially.[33]

Or again, the involvement of the kingdom of God with humanity clearly demands repentance by means of which people adopt a new way of thinking and imagining that leads to refreshing behaviors, attitudes, and conduct. Inseparably, repentance also involves others as it challenges all to make peace a reality in their daily interactions and activities with others. As it were, genuine repentance realizes itself and bears fruits in the marketplace.

In a decisive way, repentance demands that converts renounce addictive, malicious, and vicious passions that distort their perceptions and honest appraisal of human relationships. It also corrects misconceptions about God and demands that religious beliefs conform to the historical and practical demands of divine revelation in Jesus Christ.[34] Repentance that issues from faith demands that Christians believe in the God of Jesus Christ. The converted Christian finds in the ethics of discipleship that Jesus lived and proclaimed the ultimate measure of social justice. Christian justice orders human society in accordance with God's revealed will and finds that redemptive will definitively manifest in the life and teachings of Jesus.[35] Now, conversion and repentance seek to make Christians authentic disciples of Jesus Christ.

33. Ibid., 75–76.
34. Ibid., 90.
35. Ibid., 105.

DISCIPLESHIP

We do well to understand conversion by situating it within a context of Christian discipleship as a means to communion with God and fellow human beings. Christian converts grow steadily into true disciples of Jesus. To his disciples Jesus bequeathed a vision of what it means to live together as children of God in his image. Discipleship teaches the conscience to dream of a world transformed according to Jesus's moral vision and to find in God the strength and wisdom to transform that dream into an actuality. And this discipleship makes specific moral demands. The call of Christian discipleship invites and demands from Christians responses of extra creativity and generosity as well as sensitivity to conflicts and how to resolve them resourcefully.

A disciple follows Jesus in an absolute way (Mark 1:16–20; 2:13–14; 8:34–38; 10:21; 10:52; 15:40–42). According to Mark, a disciple exhibits a willingness to follow a call (Mark 1:17–18; 2:14); looks, listens, and understands (Mark 4:1–9; 4:12–13; 8:18–19; 4:20; 9:7); proclaims the good news (Mark 1:45; 3:14; 6:7–13); does the will of God (Mark 3:35; 2:23); practices fellowship and lives with the spirit of inclusiveness (Mark 9:40); and remains open to suffering for the sake of the gospel (Mark 3:34; 8:36; 10:35). A disciple does not fear Jesus; has faith and great confidence (Mark 4:40; 6:50; 8:34–35; 14:22–72; 15:42–43; 11:22; 4:39–40; 16:14); serves (Mark 9:35; 10:43–45); exercises self-denial (Mark 8:34; 10:29; 15:21); and recognizes Jesus as Son of God (Mark 15:39). A disciple rejoices at the presence of the Master and mourns during his absence (Mark 2:18–20; 14:8) and casts out demons (Mark 5:20; 6:12–13).

In Matthew, the disciple of Jesus directs himself or herself with vigilance and alert watchfulness (Matt 24:36, 51; 25:1–30; 26:36–46). Disciples also ask Jesus questions in their pursuit of understanding (Matt 13:10, 36; 15:12, 33; 17:19; 18:1, 21; 19:27; 26:18, 23, 25). Discipleship demands radical engagement (Matt 8:18, 22; 10:22, 25, 37, 39; 16:24; 18:6–9; 19:2) and focus on heavenly things (Matt 6:19–24; 6:24–34; 6:33; 7:24–27; 10:19–20; 16:23). Indeed, a disciple recognizes Christ (Matt 2:11; 14:33; 16:16; 28:17). And last but not least, a disciple can be someone of "little faith" (Matt 6:30; 8:26; 9:1; 14:31; 16:8; 17:20).

Jesus teaches his disciples to trust the Father's providential care and to present to him in prayers of petition their every need. Jesus invites his followers and disciples to prove their dedication to the kingdom of God by selling their possessions, distributing them to the poor, and joining the company of his disciples (Mark 10:21–22). This care for the poor imitates Jesus's own table fellowship with sinners and sharing bread with the needy, marginal, and outcast in order to give meaning to the great commandment (Luke 12:22–34; 16:9–13; 18:28–30). In fact, Jesus warns his disciples to mistrust wealth as a guarantee of life (Luke 12:15; 16:10–12). Moreover, massive wealth engenders a cynicism that prevents belief in the resurrection or makes such belief very difficult (Luke 16:31). In Jesus's own understanding, sharing incarnates a mutual forgiveness that measures the authenticity of a disciple's prayer (Mark 9:41; 11:25).

In the end, it must be emphasized that Jesus preached forgiveness of sins, healed the sick and possessed, and gave hope to the socially and economically disadvantaged. He also preached and lived joy, peace, justice, and love. He urged his followers to help people utilize and develop their talents and opportunities in ways that would enable people to flourish by becoming whole and free. Christian disciples form the principal vehicles for personal, interpersonal, social, and even cosmic transformation of life. Through their open-heartedness and warm-heartedness Christians help build up the world into a space of justice, love, and faith. In short, this world can become a place of grace where people consciously affirm each other's potential and give life to one another.

What is more, we have plenty of opportunities to witness to our Christian life in ways that we cannot say always remain dramatic, clear, and unquestionable. Oftentimes the rich array of invitations and appropriate moments break into our lives when we least expect them, usually in our everyday, ordinary circumstances of life. When we embrace our Christian discipleship fully, we begin to awaken to and discover our gifts, what energizes us, what provides us with the experience of joy, and what gives us deep gladness. We experience life in all its promises and potential. Thus, as we grow in discipleship, we further become mindful and cultivate the eyes that see and ears that hear Jesus, the mantle of our light that enfolds, heals, and holds us with his abundant care. In the process, God also invites us to step out of our comfort zones in faith. The resulting horizon of profound trust forms and gifts us with dispositions toward authentic living.

CONVERSION AND CHRISTIAN DISCIPLESHIP

Through justifying faith,[36] Christians find God's will normatively revealed in Jesus and in the morality of discipleship that he lived and proclaimed. This faith commits one to live as a child of God in the image of Jesus; it commits one to the ethics of faith that he proclaimed and lived. We experience initial justifying faith when we acknowledge that Jesus's religious vision claims us and the whole of humanity unconditionally and totally. The initial consent of faith yields a felt encounter with the holy.[37] It also marks the beginning of a process of personal transformation in the Spirit of Christ, who teaches us to put on his mind, attitudes, and conscience in order to transform human society according to the moral demands of life in God's kingdom.[38] God sanctifies persons by transforming them into the image of his incarnate Son through the inspiration of the Holy Spirit.[39]

Of course, one needs to note that the consent of faith emerges from the human heart's felt encounter with the one reality capable of giving human life ultimate meaning and full sense of purpose (i.e., God). The inherent beauty of that reality motivates such consent. The gift of faith transforms the pursuit of personal holiness into a form of public witness. Faith opens a person to the action of divine grace by transforming the intellect, affectivity, the conscience, and social relationships. A person of faith also shows the following traits: absolute trust in God's providential care, an all-consuming love of the God of Jesus Christ, and an unconditioned obedience to this God. That obedience entails a willingness to testify to the Risen Christ even if it means risk to one's own life. These traits free people to dedicate their lives selflessly to the service of others—that is, to share with them the material supports of life as well as the fruits and graces of the Holy Spirit. A person of faith also has a sense of his or her human limits but coupled with an absolute confidence that God will work

---

36. Justifying faith frames the experience, relationship, and insights by means of which one awakens and comes to know Jesus. It begins in the heart by confronting unhealed negative emotions that prevent a person from responding to the historical self-revelation of God in Jesus. Through justifying faith a person recognizes the beauty and excellence incarnate in Jesus and decides whether one wants to live in his image. To live in Jesus's image is to commit to live and embody his vision of the kingdom.

37. Ibid., 95.

38. Ibid., 76–77.

39. Ibid., 81.

through him or her to accomplish God's saving purposes. For the sake of Christ, a person of faith incarnates peace and tranquility.[40]

Indeed, a disciple of Jesus follows him in faith, hope, and love. In other words, growth in the theological virtues, which comes with an initial conversion, and a deepening of the conversion experience forms one more closely and clearly into the image of Jesus Christ.

CHRISTIAN CONVERSION AND GROWTH IN THEOLOGICAL VIRTUES

As the foundation of all Christian life, service, and work, the love of Christ directs the events and process of Christian conversion. And for its continual and renewed effectiveness in a given context of life, Christian conversion calls for open and candid dialogue with the appeals that the needs and demands of a given circumstance of life require. The workings of Christ in day-to-day living demand a committed and total response of the Christian in faith, hope, and love. This also, however, means that the faith, hope, and love that the Holy Spirit inspires in every converted believer manifest the Spirit's presence and saving action in a fundamental way. As a result, concrete acts of charismatic service that fail to incarnate hope, faith, and love lose their power to unite believers to God in a saving relationship.[41]

In fact, Christian conversion claims the convert totally. It demands re-evaluation, the transvaluation in faith, of all values, assumptions, and beliefs that motivate personal choices, whether affective, intellectual, or moral. Consequently, in Christian conversion the graced transvaluation of affection and perceptions leads to Christian hope. The graced transvaluation of intuitive and rational perceptions of reality leads to Christian faith while the graced transvaluation of the human conscience leads to Christian love. And the graced transvaluation of ethical concern for institutional reform motivates the Christian search for social justice.[42]

A loving and caring God who has a human face of joy and promise forms the basis of Christian hope, which also transforms natural and sinful hopes by healing, elevating, and perfecting them. Christian hope elevates natural human hopes by focusing them on the triune God. It teaches the

40. Ibid., 127–28.

41. Ibid., 80.

42. Ibid., 82.

disciples of Jesus to seek emotional healing from created remedies and ultimately, from God. Christian hope teaches the human heart to share God's own hopes for each person and for the world. In this light, it invites Christian believers to transcend the natural limitations of the human psyche: the limits of history and biology, race and sex, and class and nation. In inviting people to transcend their biases and pettiness, Christian hope sacramentalizes the human imagination; in this way, human hopes become truly liberative and humane.[43]

In healing vicious and sinful beliefs, Christian faith demands that believers in Christ perceive all created reality in God. This means that religious beliefs conform to the historical revelation of God made visible in the word incarnate. The incarnation of God provides Christians with definitive empirical evidence concerning both the reality of God and God's saving intentions in our regard.[44] The God of faith reveals and communicates God's very self. Besides, Christian faith expresses itself not just in the inferential precision of theological affirmations but also and fundamentally in ritual, narrative, myth, art, and lyric.[45]

People who seek to love others in the name and image of Jesus share their possessions with others, especially the disadvantaged or needy. People who seek to love others also reach across social and conventional barriers to the marginal and outcast, even to sinners. Their willingness to forgive measures the authenticity of their own prayer.[46] Indeed, "The mutual love of Christians for one another in the image of Jesus creates the matrix of divine grace that nurtures love in individual believers and frees them to reach out in love to others."[47] Christian charity teaches Christians to love with the forgiving love of Christ and to offer love even to those who do not merit it.[48]

CHRISTIAN DISCIPLESHIP AND CHARISMS

In inviting all to dedicate themselves to the establishment of God's just kingdom on earth as in heaven, God endows disciples with a specifically

43. Ibid., 87.
44. Ibid., 90.
45. Ibid., 93.
46. Ibid., 102.
47. Ibid., 103.
48. Ibid.

Christian character that anchors them in the exercise of some service in this world. In this light, charisms of service belong to the common patrimony of Christians. But different individuals receive and exercise different gifts. A charism exemplifies a service or ministry that the Spirit inspires members of the Christian community to exercise or perform within the community. Charisms manifest particular and graced actions of the Spirit of Christ that build up his body. A Christian charism may dedicate one to preaching wisdom, preaching instruction, faith, healing, miracles, prophecy, discernment, tongues, and interpretations of tongues. It could also dedicate one to teaching, helping, administration, almsgiving, performing works of mercy, and apostolic and pastoral leadership.[49] In short, discipleship means that when the baptized live self-centered, selfish, and pleasure-loving lives, they fall short of the practical norms and demands to which God calls them. The witness to service that the Church mediates makes the particular call of Christ, the word of God, and the sacraments efficaciously available. Without these, discipleship would in fact be hardly possible in our graced world, also scarred by sin and disorder.[50]

On the one hand, charisms arise out of the Church's creative response to the needs and direction of a given historical moment so that they nourish and build up the kingdom of God in this world. On the other hand, the metaphor of the kingdom of God originates, contextualizes, illumines, and critiques every charismatic ministry. In fact, one exercises a charism in and on behalf of the believing community called the Church. Charismatic ministry grows veritably from preaching the gospel to the world and the service of people in the light of the gospel and Jesus Christ as Lord. In this sense, through charismatic ministry God speaks and transforms history.

In effect, Christian charismatic ministry acts publicly on behalf of a Christian community to proclaim, serve, and realize the kingdom. Charismatic ministry involves more than a job; it exemplifies a vocation to serve God incarnate through the community of believers called the Church. A vocation creates a dialogue between the presence of God and one's own freedom. The exercise of all charismatic ministries presupposes God who unites, builds up, and enables the Church. In charismatic ministry, life, grace, and nature work together in a life of grace focused

49. Ibid., 125, 133.
50. Dulles, *Models of the Church*, 215–16.

upon a particular service in the community called the Church. Effective and edifying charismatic ministry involves discernment, generosity, and zeal. And the risks associated with charismatic ministry remain control, ambition, money, taste, and neurosis. This also means that an authentic charismatic ministry discerningly focuses on God continually.

The Church as a family of disciples calls attention to the ongoing relationship of the Church to Christ who continues to guide and direct it through the Holy Spirit. Together with Jesus Christ, the Church as family constitutes a contrast society, symbolically representing the new order of God's presence and the transcendent value of the kingdom of God. As a society, it breaks radically with worldly values. The community of disciples bears witness to the kingdom of God. Christian witness makes no sense apart from intense personal faith in God's providence, and in God's fidelity to his promises. Bearing witness characteristic of a disciple further requires one to appropriate redemptive suffering.[51] The grace of Christ can at times make real demands on how we respond to the issues and problems of life.

Obviously, Jesus continues to shape the community of his faithful by word and sacrament. This process entails contemplative moments since eternal life consists in knowing, believing, and rooting oneself in God and in Jesus Christ. Through God's word and sacraments the presence of Jesus among his disciples remains dynamic and affective. It transforms them into his image, claiming their lives for his service, empowering them for mission, and bearing fruit through their labors.

As an eschatological community of salvation, the Church heralds the kingdom of God. The diversity of charismatic ministries creates an organic and apostolic structure that establishes and builds up the body of the Church. Historical manifestations of charismatic ministries differ according to innate dispositions and the contextual demands of life. The apostolic origins, importance, and inevitability of charisms spring from the interplay and interface of the many tendencies and exigencies of life. It goes without saying that the Spirit guides the charismatic life of the Church historically and dynamically, individually and interpersonally. The Church's vitality roots itself in the charisms given to the community of disciples by the Holy Spirit. The generous Spirit, through charismatic ministry, creates goodness and value.

51. Ibid., 200–201.

Baptism invites all to rejoice in their identities as children of God. In this way, baptism provides a new sense of belonging by offering Christians the power to become heirs of God. Through baptism Christians enter God's family by accepting and celebrating the divine life within them. In effect, baptism comprises feeling totally loved, totally wanted, and totally accepted by God. While the identification power of Christian baptism commits a person to the lifelong process of putting on the mind of Christ, confirmation commits one to lifelong openness to the Spirit's charismatic call. Matrimonial Christian couples reaffirm their covenant of initiation in the context of taking on the responsibilities of founding a family and transforming it into a realm of saving grace. Ordination renews a Christian's covenant of initiation by accepting incorporation into the ranks of public Church leadership. All in all, ministerial offices serve the people of God.[52] Christian vocation awakens new energies and new hope that enable Christians to believe in, affirm, and trust others. In this way, they then give life to others.

When the Church as family keeps true to its mission, it maintains a historical relevance and a sense of the humanity of all people irrespective of their stations in life. It also fosters charismatic ministries and a willingness to be self-critical. Additionally, it promotes a dialogical spirit through which wholesome communication and development take place. In fact, we need to stress that the Church as family entails a web of interwoven and multi-layered relationships. This Church prolongs revelation in history. Personal being and interconnectedness constitute the very fabric of the Church's life as a life of Christian discipleship.

CONCLUSION

The Church as a communion of believers suggests brotherhood and sisterhood, the solidarity and the equality of all people as children of God. God calls the Church to provide a sanctifying presence in the world by evangelizing the world and witnessing to Christ. The metaphor of the Church as family illuminates that call. It fosters a sense of co-responsibility, dialogue, and sharing in teamwork rather than working with fiery self-isolation. The metaphor of the Church as family expresses confidence in the capacity of Christians in the community to discern the movements

---

52. Gelpi, *Committed Worship: A Sacramental Theology for Converting Christians Vol. II*, 135.

of the Spirit; it also empowers them to realize the gospel at the most basic levels of their lives.

The Church as family offers people the sense of being at home. It creates the climate where people can grow and become who they truly are as authentic persons. The Church as family can offer a desirable atmosphere of protection, security, warmth, understanding, and accepting love. The Church as a family of God builds up the house of God where believers can always find unfailing love and peace as well as the joy of forgiveness and delight as a family. Out of love, God makes himself at home in us. Our God lives, moves, and exists in and among us. We can always live where God lives, with and in him. Ultimately, God seeks presence and union. In God's blissful order of grace, we experience an active, liberating, and efficient divine presence that gives us life, energy, bonding, and unity. That presence gifts us with communication, love, belonging, and communion in the body of Christ.

The incarnation exemplifies the human embodiment of God. It unites God and human beings in the body of Jesus Christ. And so receptivity to God's offer of mercy and forgiveness in Jesus saves every dimension of the human reality.

Conversion as a life of discipleship and a deeper entry into union with God changes the center of human consciousness. It changes our orientation. Conversion centers us on the resurrected Jesus who cannot be separated from the Father and the Spirit. Conversion, in fact, fosters a deep and joyous development not reducible to acts but manifested in action and attitude. It brings about a redemptive and saving union between God and the community of believers called the Church and communion among people. In this respect, sinfulness contradicts the needs and demands of conversion.

5

The New Testament and Relational Exemplifications
of Church as Family

INTRODUCTION

THIS CHAPTER ILLUSTRATES HOW the spirit of the Church as family can actually change the way we understand, interpret, and live out the efficacy of the word of God in daily living. The spirituality of the family of God makes the words of scripture truly words of life, hope, union, reconciliation, and expansive freedom. In this way, the spirituality of the Church as family refreshes life with its sacred living message. When God becomes manifest through the words of the scriptures, we come to listen to the sacredness of our being (i.e., the sacredness of others and the self). This sacredness becomes a reality that we can concretely express, relate to, receive, and proclaim by our way of life. In so being, we establish the meaning of our lives and become capable of glorifying God.

The foregoing affirmations also mean that we respect and treat with wonder the gift of the people who come into our lives. This fact further implies that we acknowledge and connect with their sacredness so that it becomes a beautiful presence. This attitude enables us to keep loving, forgiving, and remaining open to life. The resulting joy, light, and peace recreate life with their vibrancy and greatness. The considerations of the parable of the two brothers, the appearance of the resurrected Christ to Mary Magdalene, the passion of Christ in the Gospels, the meaning of the resurrection, and the text from Paul's letter to the Romans with regard to judgmentalism serve to make clear the various manifestations of the spirituality of the Church as family. In its various expressions or manifestations this spirit unleashes, unbinds, and actualizes forces and potentials of love and bonding among people.

Christian life involves a profound existential engagement with light and the spirit of truth as necessary vehicles for gaining fundamental insights into life for communication, dialogue, and critical confidence. When we illuminate, by our very presence, the environment in which we live, we also root ourselves in the spirit of generosity and trust. Christian life roots itself in the nature and destiny of human beings in difference and nondifference as well as in the independence and transcendence of the divine mystery. Further, the subject of Christian faith corresponds to God as the symbol of inexhaustible and radical abundance that relaxes and refreshes people. The experience of God, then, leads people to liberative practices and enables them to fruitfully address the troubles that attend human contexts and communities.

Moreover, Christian faith reflects a vision of wholesome existence that involves working for the other and transcending one's own point of view, rank, and privilege. It further engages the inseparable interconnectedness between God and people, which implies living and grounding ourselves in the spiritual dimension of life and existence. This also implies living everyday life and managing limit-situations on the basis of interior life and in a spirit of the community of the Church as God's family. The following considerations variously set to explicate this reality.

LUKE 15:11–32: THE PARABLE OF THE TWO BROTHERS

At the outset, Jesus tells this story in a context where he sits with eager tax collectors and sinners who listen to his words while the Pharisees and scribes mutter and frown. Jesus tells this story to subvert our ordinary understanding and common reality, feelings, and attitudes.

In the parable we have a story of a family, but of a divided family. In this story we see workers not aware of the father but of a master. Yet the father's presence stands out. Movements of mercy, forgiveness, love, peacefulness, and life-giving warmth mark his postures. In addition, the figure of the father resonates with imposing pain and costs. It also brings out attitudes of respect and admiration, which arise from graceful responsibility and a sense of striving care. He reveals himself as full of compassion. The father understands himself as such, but the children do not. Jesus uses this parable to bridge the gap between our paradigms and the paradigms of God. In reality, no true and meaningful communication exists in this family. The questions to begin asking in this story include:

Who do we see in the house? How do the people in the house introduce themselves? Where could the young ones be? Why does the house seem like a divided family? The family does not seem to be an attractive place; it does not offer a friendly climate in which to be and grow. People in the family seem caught up in a certain business mindset. While the father understands himself as father, the children do not understand him as such. In the family that Jesus portrays in this parable, we find no meaningful sense of bonding among its members. Accordingly, the jewel of the parable lies in the fact that it aptly summarizes the complexity and troubles of our relationships with God. Thus, it represents what Jesus wanted us to know regarding our relationship with God.

The key to the parable lies with the second (older) son: the nature of his relationship with his father unlocks the basic problem between God and us. The older son in the parable says revealingly:

> Listen! For all these years I have been working like a slave for you, and I have never disobeyed your command; yet you have never given me even a young goat so that I might celebrate with my friends. But when this son of yours came back, who has devoured your property with prostitutes, you killed the fatted calf for him! (Luke 15:29–30)

The second son perceives and understands himself as a slave. He understands his relationship with his father in terms of servile obligations: "For all these years I have been working like a slave for you" (v. 29a). In effect, from the statement of the second son, we see that the father lived with a slave, albeit a loving slave. Conversely, the son declares to the father, "You were a master, a boss, to me." In effect, the other members of the family saw the father as a slave-master, even though, as the story reveals, he lived for his children and strove to hold his family together graciously and generously.

When we look at the situation of the first (younger) son, we see that he starts off on a wrong note. According to the traditions of the time, he had already killed his father, or more precisely, he had wished for the death of his father because he asked for a share of his inheritance. According to custom, a son received his portion of an inheritance after the death of his father. The younger son shared an understanding of the father similar to that of his elder brother; they shared the same identity crisis in their relationships with their father. Of the two brothers, the situation of the younger brother becomes even more critical when we understand that he had, *as a matter of fact*, two masters from his perspective: his father and his elder brother. In the story, the servants attest to the authority of his elder brother in the family: "He called one of the slaves and asked what was going on" (v. 26). In no way could the younger son win or take over masterhood in the event of his father's death. Accordingly, he eagerly sought to obtain whatever he could get from his father: "Father, let me have the share of the estate that will come to me" (v. 12).

Deep down the younger son did not believe in his sonship. He did not believe that he had been given the inheritance of a son. As a result, he feared that the father could change his mind and take back what he had given him. So, "A few days later the younger son gathered all he had and traveled to a distant country, and there he squandered his property in dissolute living" (v. 13). Away from his boss or master, the younger son could now enjoy some excitement and adventure in life. He could experience and enjoy being his own master or lord.

Now, every slave dreams of copying his master. The younger son had to go out of the context of his father, whom he perceives as his master, in order that he himself can be a master. He wanted to enjoy the rank of lord and master somewhere. But the experience of being lord and master did not last very long, for "he had spent everything" (v. 14a). He lost all his inheritance. In fact, his decline and fall took place rather fast. He then tasted the real experience and meaning of servitude: "He went and hired himself out to one of the citizens of that country, who sent him to his fields to feed the pigs" (v. 15). As his situation deteriorated and became pathetic, he actually surrendered as a slave, "And he would willingly have filled himself with the husks the pigs were eating but no one would let him have them" (v. 16). He became someone reduced to a state of desiring to eat with the pigs, the cursed creature associated with demons. In the younger son, then, we see a being who has nowhere to rest. He becomes a symbol of a deeply restless being. He reached the bottom-line. He experienced and lived in isolation, fragility, homelessness, and insecurity.

He reached rock bottom, a situation of no options or of *apparent* no exit. He lost self-respect, dignity, and self-identity. He had little or no choice about his situation. This experience embodies and brings forth an image of hell. In fact, he became desperate. He found himself at the end of his tether. But this experience awakened him to a new sense or consciousness of himself. The text says, "But when he came to himself he said, 'How many of my father's hired hands have bread enough and to spare, but here I am dying of hunger!'" (v. 17).

The younger son awakened to the consciousness of being a son. He awakened to, identified with, and accepted the responsibility that comes with the honor of sonship. He began to act according to the conscience of a son. And for the first time he used the words of a son and meant what he said. His tragedy became a blessing of the highest quality. The experience opened for him a new and different paradigm that brought him new perspectives. For the first time, he used the word father to mean father and not lord and master. He further realized a stage of differentiation: he could distinguish between son, workers (hired hands), and brothers. His situation of no options forced out his true identity. This amazing experience coincided with the emergence of a new self-identification and self-definition.

Oftentimes tragedy or limitations of life force people to face the truth of who they truly are as persons. Often people continue to live in falsehood until faced with pain, crisis, trauma, or adversity. In other words, God keeps tracking us wherever we go until one time we have nowhere to go so that we may have the *Abba experience* as a liberative, transforming experience of self-discovery and wakefulness to who we truly are. The *Abba experience*, which coincides with the human experience of the highest possible quality, transfigures our life with its radiance, positivity, and excellence. The *Abba experience* implies irrevocably that God likes us. He loves us. He trusts and enjoys us. God likes to be with us. He wants it. He enjoys it. This experience enables us to receive ourselves from ourselves in spontaneous acts of giving and sharing.

With a new consciousness of his own identity as son, the younger son made a plan to return. He also became conscious of his own sinfulness. Simultaneously, thus, the consciousness of being a son came with his sense of sinfulness. Further, he had to face the insults, contempt, shame, and humiliation that would come with an embarrassing return to his father's house. As a result, he decided to legally become a servant. This experience matches up with the self-emptying of Jesus; in fact, it coincides with Jesus's experience in its true and eternal depths. Consequently, the younger son declared, "I will get up and go to my father, and I will say to him, 'Father, I have sinned against heaven and before you; I am no longer worthy to be called your son; treat me like one of your hired hands'" (vv. 18–19).

Where identity disorder exists, everything turns on its head. The sin connected with our identity affects everything about us. This sin, as manifested in this story, for instance, masks the father with the category of lord and master. It further disfigures the positive desire to become like the father (i.e., our striving to become divine). The desire, in fact, becomes a complex. But Jesus, through this story, also discloses a father who transcends legalism. Only the consciousness of being son or daughter matters to the father in the narrative:

> But while he was still far off, his father saw him and was filled with compassion; he ran and put his arms around him and kissed him. Then the son said to him, "Father, I have sinned against heaven and before you; I am no longer worthy to be called your son." But the father said to his slaves, "Quickly, bring out a robe—the best one—and put it on him; put a ring on his finger and sandals on his feet. And get the fatted calf and kill it, and let us eat and celebrate; for this son of mine was dead and is alive again; he was lost and is found!" And they began to celebrate. (vv. 20b–24)

The scene depicted above communicates a symbolism rich with meanings. We see that the father went and met the younger son long before anyone else; the younger son risked abuse, humiliation, rejection, and possible banishment. And the actions of the father cut short the words of the son. His actions did not allow the younger son to say his prepared speech and call himself a hired servant. The father's actions recognized and proclaimed unmistakably the son's identity, which transcended that of hired men—namely, sonship. The father welcomed him as a true son of the family. The father did not care why he returned. Rather, he cared that he had come back. Thereafter the feast began.

God comes all the way to meet us. Also, in the story the father pays for all the costs. He does most of the speaking. And when he speaks he simply states his worry and expresses his feelings. He states his anguish and his joy. He celebrates and glorifies his identity as a father. And he helps the son to celebrate his identity. The father does not point a finger. The ring he puts on the finger of his younger son signifies, "You are my own self, my own likeness." The fattened calf symbolizes that "everything we have been doing must be brought out to celebrate the new consciousness of sonship," a newly discovered sense of identity. For God, all and everything carries little or no value except in relationship to bringing up the identity of his son or daughter. This attitude contrasts sharply with a business mind. What we own or do cannot be commensurate with our identity as sons and daughters of God. All property has value only as a vehicle for celebrating our identities of being sons and daughters of God. They ought to help us be more and more who we can become as authentic beings. The meaning of our relationship with God consists in this big celebration of our identity.

The father also says, "Son, you are always with me, and all that is mine is yours" (v. 31). In this way, God anchors the whole salvation and liberation of the world in each one of us. The whole world seems to reside in us, for better or for worse. All we can attribute to God we should be able to attribute to ourselves. As it were, "All the Father is I am." The human being has enormous and abundant riches within that can be discovered, grasped, shared, and expanded through being. In other words, we exceed all we do, feel, know, seek, and have or the organizations or communities to which we belong. We can always affirm and develop the spiritual and divine dimension of our being and in so doing, enrich tremendously our identities and lives. When we root ourselves in being, the experience offers us a secure, peaceful, empowering, and liberating type of lively identity. This also, however, means that we find in ourselves a blending of our being with that of Christ, which enhances and invigorates a balanced and available sense of self. As a result of this blending, connection with others becomes existential and enjoyable as we continually experience ourselves as significant and self-accepting.

Divinity and Ourselves

All the authority the father has, we have. Our shame cannot be separated from the shame of God, our parent. We form one body: we either survive or we die together. In other words, our salvation touches on improving the quality of our lives together, which involves incremental adjustments that enable us to face and constructively cope with the demands of life. We do not achieve wholeness through the mechanisms of survival of the fittest. United we float, divided we sink. Ordinarily, this truth contrasts with the wisdom of everyday conventional life. Yet God has nothing except with us. God remains so inasmuch as he begot us. He shares himself, his own life, to beget us into his own image.

In other words, God has chosen humanity as his viable medium for effecting his salvation. Therein exist the blessing and blessedness of being human. God saves in human ways (i.e., through human hearts, imagination, eyes, hands, and ears). We have the capacity to receive and express the presence of God and his kingdom in the world. God works in the world in human ways. Thus, true human transformation and liberation require not only dedication and refined technical approaches, but they also call for a genuine spirit of cooperation among people of goodwill on behalf of the common good of humanity. When we put forth generous and far-sighted efforts that embody enduring values that honor the integral wellbeing of one another, we improve the quality of our life together. Such efforts also include cultivating habits of responsible decision-making rooted in the appreciation of truth and justice that at once also marks the beginning of sympathy and compassion.

Who we authentically become derives from God sharing his own life with us. God does not simply deal with us as he would act on objects. Instead God's activities empower and invite us to act in liberating ways. As a matter of fact, we determine how we act and respond to life situations. As subjects, we co-create with God through our acts. In short, God does not own us. We come from the same stuff or stock of God. In the book of Genesis we have: "then the LORD God formed man[1] from the dust of the ground, and breathed into his nostrils the breath of life; and the man became a living being" (Gen 2:7).

Every human being symbolizes and embodies a concrete instance of the living God among us. We form part and parcel of God. We remain, in a certain sense, begotten and not made. Our exciting life comes from God's own very self. God's personal and inner life connects and bonds with our unique, authentic selves. In this way, God delivers, affirms, and renews our being. Gen 1:27 clearly presents it thus: "So God created humankind in his image, in the image of God he created them; male and female he created them." Human-created reality does not stand nor give life on its own without the breath of God (i.e., without sharing in the Spirit of God).

---

1. Some scholars make a big issue of the biblical translation that uses the word *man* to denote a human being, male and female. But anyone who knows the history of English language knows that in Old English and Anglo-Saxon, the suffix –*man* was gender-neutral. It had and still retains the same meaning as person today, referring to all people equally. To denote gender it needed qualification so that a male was called a *waepman*, a female *wifman*. This gender-free use of –*man* gives forms like *chairman, fisherman, craftsman*, meaning a person of either sex who engages in a given work or profession. It then turns out that the supposed ancient sexist meaning enshrined in the word, in fact, does not exist. See Hughes, *Culture of Complaint*, 22.

The Spirit of God in us feeds on the earth, which forms part of who we have become. As embodied spiritual beings on a human journey, we remain part of this earthly life. At the same time, the physical world does not coincide with the part of our identity that partakes of God's. Certainly, God owns the universe insofar as he created it.

As Christians, if we follow Jesus step by step, what we attribute to God we can attribute to ourselves. Subsequently, we have to say that the divinity of God refers to God as Father and Mother to all. We confirm divinity when we become brothers and sisters to all, which sense of kinship includes all generations or at least wishes them well. It also implies our readiness and willingness to forgive one another. To practice divinity means to build up and make possible the community of the disciples of Christ as the family of God. The practice of divinity takes place in a Eucharistic community where members have voices, celebrate the joy of living, and share warm-heartedness with one another.

Celebrating divinity can embarrass us with its challenges. To practice divinity implies and goes beyond humor and amusement. Joy in celebrating our divine origin and identity constitutes the true goal of our lives. We cannot imagine God truly without the sense and experience of the common inheritance of all. The experience of the *all in all* engenders extraordinary joy. In this light, the issue of reconciliation also becomes very crucial in the Christian and human enterprise. The family of God must be re-united at any cost, including the cost of unconditional acceptance, mercy, and forgiveness. So, the key invitation of life becomes the task of renaming, gathering, and reconciling all the scattered children of God in God's family.

The difficulty of celebrating divinity reveals itself in the story through the words of the elder son:

> Listen! For all these years I have been working like a slave for you, and I have never disobeyed your command; yet you have never given me even a young goat so that I might celebrate with my friends. But when this son of yours came back, who has devoured your property with prostitutes, you killed the fatted calf for him! (vv. 29–30)

In speaking of "this son of yours," the older brother, in effect, makes clear that he too left the family even though he remained physically in it. He had not truly identified with the family so that he could not fully participate in some of its most intimate and key elements in the family aching drama. He had excluded himself from one of its cherished experiences—namely, the loss of a member. He had no sense of the father's continual love, intentions, and desires for the younger son and family togetherness that includes all. He did not understand the father's feelings, cares, and dream of holding and bonding the family together. In a sense, then, the older brother betrayed a certain lack of love of the father. He did not share truly in the passion of the father. Further, his self-righteousness threatened to weaken, dissipate, and even rupture the experience of reconstituting the family bond once again.

The older son saw what the father did to the younger son as an installation of his younger brother's lordship and masterhood. In the slave mindset or mentality, one can only become a master or a slave/servant. Conversely, the elder brother saw an entrenchment of his servanthood or slavehood. Conceivably, he might plan how to overthrow and perhaps eliminate his younger brother so that the story could end on a very sad note. After all, the older brother resented the father's actions and love for the younger brother. Precisely, the luminous acceptance and forgiveness shown by the father remained amazing and incredible to the older brother.

The elder son did not discover the father's love as the younger son did. In fact, as the narrative goes, the younger son did not go back on his discovery. Disturbingly, then, we do not know from the story whether the elder son went into the celebration or not. This means also, however, that we do not have to go into the feast. We each have to make our own decisions. We have to take a step; we have to make a decision by discerning what God asks of us at a given moment of our life. Therein lies the meaning of coming to our senses. God wants to be with us. God wants us to grow enough into union with him so that we may live the power of our divine identity as the identity of our own truth as persons. We achieve this new, great identity by accepting the divine life within us. This identification power makes us become heirs of God through the life of baptism. When we honor and respect our divine identity we come back to the house of the Father.

Part of the Christian calling consists of celebrating, sharing, and enjoying our divine identity as a free gift of God. This identity also means that God totally wants, accepts, and loves each one of us. The Christian proclamation refers to making known the fact that divine sonship and daughterhood exist for all or more precisely, are open to all. This proclamation invites all to recognize, rejoice in, and trust their identities as true children of God. Only in this relationship do we have an enduring experience and sense of existential security, confidence, peace, and wellbeing.

Revealingly, the mother does not feature in the story involving a father and his two sons. Did she become one of the workers in the family perhaps? Had she become one of the servile handmaids? While we may not answer these questions with definiteness, we can understand the absence of the mother. In fact, the motherhood of God seems the most victimized and probably the least-acknowledged and -respected aspects of divinity. When we behave like slaves in relation to God we force God to put on the garb of lord and master. All aspects of gentleness, patience, kindness, and tenderness (what many cultures conventionally regard as motherly qualities) cannot come out. So, had there been a mother's love, could that younger brother have found a reason to stay home?

The tasks and responsibility of the slave consist in praising the lord or master with all his or her energies so that he or she has very little energy to love the self. In fact, no person hates himself or herself like a salve. Even love of neighbor carries little meaning to a slave since he or she does not truly love himself. In effect, terrible interactions tend to happen between slaves; they can inflict unimaginable misery and death on one another as they undercut and degrade one another to unprecedented levels.

Therefore, the greatest injustice we can do to ourselves consists in not discovering and knowing who we are, namely our identities as sons and daughters of God and as brothers and sisters of the same quality. For in so being, we fail to respect our rank. We cannot be and develop ourselves in freedom and joy in ways that let others be themselves joyfully. In telling this story Jesus tells us how to liberate not only ourselves but God as well. If we cannot reclaim our true identity, we cannot let God be truly God. The liberation of humanity and divinity comes about when we truly celebrate our identities as sons and daughters of God together.

In fact, people generally initiate their children into society through the paradigm of earthly lordship. Competition, success, and language facilitate and reinforce the foothold that this paradigm gains in our lives. Many cultural processes of socialization frequently lead to the man becoming master and lord and the woman becoming a slave of the man. Subsequently, as it often happens like it happened to the younger son, the man begins to experience disillusionment and emptiness. He realizes that others only glorify and love what he does and what he has. Nobody really loves his person. This realization often leads to an experience of a felt emptiness, an escape from which may express itself in drinking, loss of discipline, and irresponsibility. Things begin to fall apart, as the man increasingly loses his self-respecting sense of honor, glory, and shame. Further degeneration leads to loss of the sense of shame and glory.

For the woman, meanwhile, the experience of enslavement can lead to an experience of a different variety of disillusionment. She realizes that the man needs her because of her service—that is, out of his need for her and not for who she is. Through this realization the woman can begin to lose her sense of care and responsibility. In her own way, she badly searches for control or genuine love through means fraught with missteps and inattention to possible risks. The often-resulting frightful consequences make it difficult to initiate and sustain healthy relationships. Of course, the depiction of what occurs to a man could happen to a woman and vice-versa. In the end, a relationship of servility always leads to destruction while a relationship of unity and freedom of the children of God engenders and spreads life and joy.

Continuously, everyone requires a new birth. This often entails stripping oneself of what one has accumulated. For only in this way can we truly root ourselves in our identity as sons and daughters of God and brothers and sisters to others with whom we can walk together. Our dignity comes with the gift of our being; we do not earn our dignity. The meaning of living the baptism of fire through God's grace consists in realizing the consciousness of our enduring identity and dignity. When we live as sons and daughters of God we radiate that same spirit and life of God.

The Passion of Christ in the Gospels and Our Humanity

At one level, the passion represents the terrifying gift and responsibility to choose according to our own conscience. It also implies the courage to accept the obligation to choose according to our identities as sons and daughters of God.

In the passion narratives, the arrest of Jesus frustrates him; he cannot move freely as he used to. He bore the accusation of being a revolutionary, a heretic, a blasphemer, and basically an atheist. The passion put his own reputation at stake and called into question his whole ministry and work. The warm, friendly presence of Jesus became poignant, though he remained calm for the most part. He continued to be tender, tenacious, and faithful in the face of impending calamity.

In light of his situation, he accepted the risk of losing the protection of his followers, the apostles. In fact, Judas Iscariot betrayed him. He allowed Judas to remain by his side 'til the last betrayal. He accepted him and respected his dignity. The three disciples he took with him to the garden of Gethsemane fell asleep at his hour of need. Some of his disciples fled, and the Apostle Peter denied him. They could not watch him in such pain; they could not understand. His own disciples had not seen him in this way before. It was a new experience for them. They could not be sure that they would not be arrested; they did not want to be arrested. In short, Jesus was let down by his most intimate friends. Therein lay the depth of his pain.

Jesus also accepted the risk of losing the protection of the rulers who actually condemned him to death. Religious leaders incited the people against him. In effect, he lost the support of the ordinary people even when Pilate made some effort to try to release him. In fact, they clamored for the release of a brigand in preference to him. What is more, he even felt abandoned by the presence of His father. He died with a loud cry, but he did not surrender to death. He remained faithful to the Father. He trusted God even amidst many experiences of strangeness, cruelty, disconcertion, and a feeling of unknown darkness. He still experienced being one with God in the depths of his heart. He handed himself to his Father; the definitive word of love remained his last utterance. He made his final choice out of love (i.e., having more confidence in God than in himself). He did not lose the hope of entering into the kingdom of joy.

No doubt, Jesus tasted the full bitterness of human limitations during his passion. He drank the chalice of piercing disappointment, wounding doubt, stinging pain, and dispiriting despair. The passion then leaves us with a picture of Jesus who remains alone, powerless, without support, and without a breath of life. In this way, Jesus experienced the basic poverty of being human in the adventure of realizing human salvation. Interestingly, too, we must note that love always generates impulse and movement; it also involves struggle, creativity, risk, and fatigue. Love has a dimension of freedom. In this regard, Jesus respected the freedom of his people. He submitted to the cross rather than compel them to accept his message of salvation. Herein lies an important insight: true freedom, which starts from love and faith, begins where another's freedom starts.

At the passion Jesus shared his own life. His human identity was the one thing that remained with him—his being the Son of God. God shared his own life to make us more conscious of our identity as sons and daughters of God and thereby learning new orientation of life. Only God can liberate us from ourselves and gather us together so that we become more fully alive. This fact also means that there always remains an aspect of mystery in us and in our relationships with one another. We have elements of trust, faith, charity, and hope in us and all that we are. Charity means the continual unveiling of the desirability, attractiveness, and lovableness of all people. And where inequality exists we find potential violence at play so that inequality touches on matters of life and death.

The passion means that when we ultimately make our final choices out of love we unbind ourselves. We also actualize genuine freedom by means of which we retain our dignity as well as that of others. And as free persons we do not readily yield to the temptation of power. So, the love that bears us through the passion looks beyond the struggle for justice; it looks for a totally different world. In love we develop an immeasurable bond with life and freedom that unleashes our creativity and involvement in the world. But the power of this freedom truly comes from attachment to God and God alone.

The passion of Christ teaches radically that we cannot lose God since nobody can manipulate God. This fact also means that we remain always stronger than anything others can do to us. The God of liberty lives within us. Others can take away from us only what we want to give or what we are ready to lose or let go. In the circumstances, spiritual freedom or liberty (i.e., inner freedom) implies possessing nothing so as to leave room to receive everything. This reality also means that we do not idolize, for example, career, power, money, reputation, prestige, friendship, and conditional external security. We then accept the risk to lose everything. Paradoxically, the strong become those who have nothing to lose or who do not fear to lose what they have in fact. Such freedom of the strong arises, for the Christian, from the love and faith in the living and resurrected Christ.

Thus, spiritual freedom coincides with the gift of life from which we cannot simply walk away. It means responsibility for life and freedom from fear, freedom from legalism, and freedom from death. But we struggle and work for such freedom. In fact, we have to keep working for it since it is not a one-off experience. Through spiritual freedom we fulfill the most secret urgings of our consciences and humanity. We satisfy our longing for the ultimate fuller life by means of which we further have creative influence on particular histories. In this way, the baptized live more fully their baptismal commitment that particularly expresses itself in service and self-sacrifice, especially for those in need. In any case, when we experience interior freedom we can love always.

Spiritual freedom also finds decisive expression in the nonacceptance of the desperate search for domination and the refusal of manipulation and of sexuality separated from love. It also does not submit to the exigencies of isolation and alienation. This freedom further implies openness and willingness to live with risks, unpopularity, insecurity, and loss of prestige and privileges, comfort and peace of mind. In any case, love implies the openness to take risks and a journey to an unknown and a different world; in love we leave the familiar in order to go where we do not know. Love believes that the future offers possibilities of new and wondrous discoveries. Hence, love urges us outward and transforms our life with a sense of joyful discovery. In this way, love recreates us. In love the only legitimate fear becomes not being able to attain that which we aspire toward and yet which we believe belongs to our heritage and which would bring us fulfillment.

In effect, love overcomes fears and uncertainties. When we experience insecurity it often means that we do not feel certain. We then lose hope in others and in ourselves. This fact also means that we cannot bear the price tags of misunderstanding, exile, persecution, and martyrdom. In fear, we normally become afraid to lose something. In contrast, love does not mind giving up things; it wants to give out rather than hold back. Accordingly, it cannot be strongly emphasized enough that it requires some depth of love to go on living or go through insecurity, struggle, and fatigue—that is, not to let fears paralyze us, not to lose hope, and to continue to build up a creative world of human fellowship. In the process, we learn to free ourselves from the old and familiar by accepting the new and wondrous.

The passion of Christ then implies that we continually strip our interior selves of all power, honor, glory, and things we own. These extrinsic attractions and standards cannot be sources of lasting happiness, as they lead repeatedly to disillusionment. God truly shares his own life at the passion to make us more conscious of our identity as sons and daughters of God. The passion entails learning a new orientation for wholesome joy.

Only God, in this way, can bring us back through a liberation of ourselves and a gathering of all people as brothers and sisters. This also means, however, that unity, peace, and reconciliation, based on equality in dignity, responsibility, and opportunities, can make us more fully alive. Living the gospel then implies living by appeal, goodness, reconciliation, and example. The human and Christian call requires that we love one another to the point of dying for each other.

When we appropriate the unconditional worth of our persons we develop confidence in ourselves, by becoming aware of ourselves and drawing from our deepest resources, energies, and the task of living. The resulting self-acceptance also means embracing weaknesses, limitations, relativity of things, and opening ourselves up to the future with trust and hope. As we assume responsibility for our own destiny, we give shape to our lives with dedication and a measure of self-forgetfulness as we accept witnesses without undue fears. We come to embody a mysterious source of courage and conviction. We also live with trust by maintaining a relationship of generosity and gratuity.

In the circumstances, we can speak with each other with affectionate honesty and genuine respect. This also means that we live open, interested, and friendly lives that inspire and encourage generous determination. Certainly, all this calls for a great deal of interior negotiation, which needs psychological steadfastness and spiritual resources of sorts.

JOHN 20:11–18: THE APPEARANCE OF JESUS TO MARY MAGDALENE

Jesus's teaching and message on how we need to live in the family of God reveals itself further in his appearance to Mary of Magdala. In the first place, Mary looked for Jesus everywhere, even to the garden. She wanted to perform her last service. After all, she had experienced Jesus being dead. But in this story, Mary, at one level, preoccupied herself with her lord and master who died. When asked by the angels why she wept, she said, "They have taken away my Lord, and I do not know where they have laid him" (v. 13). The absence of her lord and master deeply disoriented her. She looked for a dead lord and buried master. Because she could not find him, her heart broke. Her prevailing disposition blinded her completely to the unfolding and new reality before and around her. She could not see anything or truth outside her mindset or existing frame of mind.

Interestingly, the angel (which means one who resembles God) did not impress her. Her search for her lord and master framed her all-consuming desire. The angels did not seem to relate with her as lords or masters, so they did not interest her. She continued to look for what she wanted, but she did not find it. Her paradigm of the lordship-servant and master-slave relationship fixed and blinded her. She could not make sense of any relationship outside that paradigm.

The attitude of Mary further revealed something interesting. When she encountered Jesus in the course of her frenetic search, she wanted to cling to him in a characteristic way of the master and his slave. Mary's clinging attitude prompted Jesus to tell her, "Do not hold on to me, because I have not yet ascended to the Father. But go to my brothers and say to them, 'I am ascending to my Father and your Father, to my God and your God'" (v. 17). Mary sought possessive attachment to Jesus as would be proper in a relationship between a lord and his servant. But Jesus wanted a different relationship, and Jesus helped her come out of old and now-fake veils of reality. A whole new world was set up in which Jesus revealed himself as alive. As with Mary, the joy and power of the encounter with the resurrected Christ sends us out to other people so that we can share the good news as a liberating experience with them.

What is more, Jesus established a new way of relating with him. Mary could now only relate with him personally in faith (i.e., through belief). This also means that even those who have not seen him physically can relate with him provided they believe in him (i.e., share in the resurrection faith). In encountering Mary in the garden, a place and symbol of new creation, the living and resurrected Jesus, in effect, installed and definitively established a new paradigm by which he wanted his friends, brothers, and sisters to know and proclaim him. Decidedly, Jesus revealed himself as *a brother* when he said, "Go to my brothers and say to them" (v. 17b). In the encounter with Mary, Jesus did not stay long. After a little while with Mary, he went on. But the encounter brought immense consolation and joy to Mary (v. 18). Simultaneously, Jesus also disclosed God as Father when he said, "I am ascending to my Father and your Father, to my God and your God" (v. 17c). This revelational paradigm of brotherhood, fellowship, fraternity, and kinship among people *through faith* truly coincides with the depth of *familyhood*. Jesus's whole mission had been a process of de-legitimizing the paradigm of lordship-servitude from human relations.

The Resurrection and Human Relationships

In fact, the passion of Jesus stripped him of all aspects of worldly lordship. At his death he had nothing left. At death he bore no trace or evidence of earthly lordship. He did not even own his own body. He had even given away his mother and his spirit. At his death, he owned nothing. He died alone and in utter powerlessness. People could comfortably mock and ridicule him without fear of any reprisal. With his death, he de-legitimated human lordship and masterhood. People turned him into a faked lord whom they could mock and ridicule.

Jesus's witness did not involve any visible glory, honor, or power. People spat on him. He died between a thief and a murderer. He died naked. His followers abandoned and denied him. Paradoxically, when people stripped Jesus of all the external trappings of earthly lordship, the truth of his person came out: *he revealed himself as the Son of God; for this he came and died.* As it were, the last word rested with the revelation of his sonship in relation to God the Father. In Mark 15:36–37, we have a testimony from a centurion, a non-Jew, that the manner of Jesus's death revealed his divine sonship:[2]

> Then Jesus gave a loud cry and breathed his last. And the curtain of the temple was torn in two, from top to bottom. Now when the centurion, who stood facing him, saw that in this way he breathed his last, he said, "Truly this man was God's Son!"

In its most primary meaning, lordship coincides with sovereignty. Accordingly, the lordship of Jesus, as the experience and expression of his own sovereignty in life, springs from his interior liberty. The lordship of Jesus that does not depend on ownership, control, and fear has its basis in deep spiritual freedom that inveighs against any way, shape, or form of loading it over others. The lordship of Jesus testifies against earthly masterhood. His lordship simultaneously signifies filial trust, actual sacrifice, concrete love, and lived justice in the sense of right relationships among people. This lordship does not depend on honor and appearances; rather, it communicates itself through forms of righteousness, peace, and joy by means of which all access the banquet of human fellowship and the full life.

---

2. In this way, the lordship of Jesus de-legitimized all earthly lordship. He is lord but in a different sense.

The passion was not the end for Jesus. Surely, the passion did not offer meaning in life. Jesus's resurrection did. The Father raised Jesus up to new and everlasting life. In a deep way, the resurrection means that we remain stronger and greater than any created human structure, than any programmed extermination, than any experience of alienation or tyranny. We always remain spiritual beings learning to live in a human way. The resurrection confirms God's promise to make all things new.

In the experience of the resurrection we find the guarantee that our life is meant for freedom to love forever in unlimited ways. When we love we expand ourselves in relationships, we expand in maturity, and we grow to understand our dependence on God and our own limits. A beautiful realization thus happens. This fact also means, however, that we have already begun to rise from the dead and always remain called to life even though the question of death may remain unresolved in certain ways. Victory belongs to life and not to death even though death may still stalk us, our neighborhoods, our streets, our villages, our towns, our countries, and our various regions of the world. We have hope; we have reason to hope even though evil still shares in a lot of ways the same table of life with goodness. And true human creativity entails a commitment to the liberation of all. Love remains the greatest expression of the total gift of self.

God lives within us to make us discover what genuine life really is. He arouses within us the desire for communion with Him. In this, the experience of connecting with God from within, we experience the joy of living that imbues us with genuineness and prophetic power in our normal, everyday living. Christ only asks us for faith in him—that we believe in him and that we shall rise again. God remains the God of freedom and brother to us all, especially the exploited and oppressed. Christ has won a victory; our task remains that of carrying it on. We are called to divine destiny, which also implies the process as an ongoing adventure.

Because Christ rose from the dead, we can now worship in spirit and truth. The resurrection constitutes the starting point for humanity's march toward a world that is different and unknown, a beautiful, exciting, and wonderful world that has an irresistible appeal and charm of the untouched and unsullied. The resurrection is cause for deep joy and a great inner security. We can now become involved in the world in a freed, creative, and joyful way. We liberate our being with the element of joy. We liberate ourselves from all that poisons the wonder of living:

selfishness and greed, hatred and revenge, pride and possessiveness, victory and dominance, impotence and stupidity. We liberate ourselves from inner disorder that comes from evil thoughts, desires, and imagination. Through the resurrection God provides us with a good life insurance (i.e., an assurance of a continuation of worthwhile life and living hope).

As a result, we experience moral and spiritual liberation. We then move toward peace, love, and fulfillment as gifts of the Holy Spirit that the risen Christ bestows on us: "Receive the Holy Spirit. If you forgive the sins of any, they are forgiven them; if you retain the sins of any, they are retained" (John 20:22b–23). Grace is not given once; it is given every day. Once God has given it to us, he wants it every day. Peace as a gift of the Holy Spirit arises from a sense of assurance that comes with accepting and reverencing God's love and security. When we trust and embrace a provident God, a powerful and gentle God of active and efficient love who is always there, we experience and express lived peace. The resurrection makes us a giving people of hope. This also means that we have to be the people of Jesus by the way we live. The invitation of hope lies in believing in the kingdom of joy and in living as if it were already a reality. As it were, we taste a transforming moment of true, simple, and serene delight. In this way, we become what we believe; we produce spirituality.

The resurrection cannot be separated from responsibility for life born of love and faith in Christ. It also entails respect for the development of others, respect for the dignity of all, and accepting all without discrimination. All this further implies openness to the impulse to trust God, openness to the gentle presence of goodness, openness to truth, openness to mercy and compassion, openness to union and love, and openness to new life and light. To behold the mystery of God in the resurrection means to stay with God. It is staying with meaning, dimensions, and perspectives of life that we cannot wholly grasp. It is to continue believing, loving, and hoping. When we honor, accept, and embrace God's reality and presence we create a sacred covenant with him. We then achieve personal centering and loving fellowship with one another. Our covenant with God gives us life and the impetus, courage, and struggle against forms of injustice and oppression so that we build up a freer and more humane world. In true loving fellowship, we believe in the originality of each person. We respect the consciences of others. We also commit ourselves to every demand of justice without hating anyone.

The achievable sacred ordering with God, with others, and with ourselves produces peace. Or again, when we actuate and awaken the presence and gifts of the living God within and among us, we establish a new order of the joy of peace. This joy of peace coincides with the joy of our participation in the life of the resurrection. Then we realize that this life truly makes sense, that its horizon opens into light and promise.

The God of Jesus Christ

As noted earlier, in the encounter with Mary, Jesus reveals himself as a *brother* and God as a *Father*. The God he talks about has nothing except what he has together with us. If we do not cooperate with him, he can do nothing. Our God has no power, no honor, and no glory except the one that he has with us as his sons and daughters. In this light, Jesus only promises one thing: to be with us in everything that happens to us as a brother.

Jesus Christ promises us his companionship. He does not promise to defend and protect us from struggles and suffering. He pledges to remain with us through all our experiences. This Jesus Christ coincides with one who witnesses to his identity as Son of the Father who coincides with the source of all goodness. This Jesus suffers as Son of the Father. He strives to be good and continually strives to remain a source of all goodness. He also desires and wishes that his disciples and all people of goodwill become sources of all goodness. His disciples share in his mission and suffering inasmuch as they witness to their identities as sons and daughters of the Father. In short, witnessing to his identity and the identities of all people as brothers and sisters of the same quality typified all of Jesus's attitudes, activities, and directions in life.

Thus, the main thing about God has to do with his solidarity with us in all our ways: shame, suffering, joys, and hopes 'til the end of time. God's love has to do with *his being with us*. God expects us to be always with him and with one another as brothers and sisters. True worship means being with one another, which has reconciliation and forgiveness as vital aspects and resources of life. This experience truly corresponds to and epitomizes the *good news*. The risk we face in this task and calling lies in the fact that we can condition our response to the mystery of God and one another, in which case mystery cannot reveal itself as such. We can force mystery to reveal itself differently to us. In fact, if we do not exercise great care with our language and disposition, we force Jesus to reveal himself in no other way than as lord. We can do similarly with each other.

Now, God does not generate us in the same way that a machine produces its products. Otherwise we would be mere tools and instruments in the hands of God. Our worth would depend on our utility so that without use we would cease to be anybody or anything. Intrinsically, we become nothing, or more precisely, worth nothing. We could only be good instruments so that we would begin to refer to ourselves only in terms of use. And God would love us as long as we remained his good instruments. God's love would only be utilitarian. Such love would also be conditional. Within this context, hell becomes a dumping place for those who have become bad tools and deserve disposal and perhaps destruction. In this same vein, religion itself becomes destructive. People who cannot be good tools cannot come close to God. The weak and disabled or disadvantaged come to find no meaningful place in religion. Religion becomes a preserve of the strong, the powerful, and the intelligent. In the last analysis, all relationships become utilitarian, temporal, and empty of any lasting significance. To relate with another would inevitably imply these questions: How can I use you? What can I get from you? You are important only as long as I can use you. What use do you have for me? Can I be of use to him or her?

Subsequently, life and existence become a matter of survival. This means that a person who interferes with another's mode of survival in life risks serious reactions or even physical elimination as survival determines the consciences and actions of people. Fear of God only comes to matter insofar as it remains a means of sustaining one's survival. God remains God as long as he guarantees survival. Otherwise God loses relevance and people disregard him. Or again, God exists, moves, lives, and loves insofar as he guarantees survival. People reverence and acknowledge God in their lives on the condition that God offers, maintains, and extends modes of their survival. The resulting conditional spirituality becomes one of spying on what makes the other succeed in life. In the circumstances, worship of God cannot take place in spirit and truth.

Survival also interpolates itself between human relationships. This means that an economic or financial item or commodity interferes with and in fact blurs the intrinsic worth of human relationships. To own all things becomes a critical value for which people can blackmail, abuse, and attack each other. Humanity truly loses its intrinsic value.

As a result, people inflict much damage and suffering on one another. Weapons, money, and might become very important tools for survival. To this list one could also add the conceptual and perceptual arsenals of collective defense. Makers of tools of survival also become very powerful leaders in the human community. Property ownership then results in hierarchical or hegemonic order as well as obedience by servants, workers, employees, or slaves. The lord becomes the one who owns all or more things in a given relationship. The human self surrenders to possession or the mode of possessing. The lord owns all power, honor, praise, and glory. In the end, we develop a relationship of slavery among people. Religiously, the consequences become horrendous. Divinity becomes interpreted in terms of lordship, ownership, word (command) and obedience, and ranking. Socially, celebrating life becomes a celebration of ranks (i.e., a ritual of acknowledging the pecking order in human relations). Love becomes conditional, enslaving, and fake, for it directs itself not to a person but to what a person has or does. The motivation for love becomes fear of punishment and expectation of reward. A good lord also becomes an adept tyrant.

As human relationships compete for favors, people begin to deal with one another through jealousy and envy as well. In the circumstances, the blessing of one person easily becomes the curse of another. What should bring joy engenders various levels of malice, intrigues, and resentment. People step on one another and stab each other in the back. By the same token, people craft arguments because they deem them strategic to achieving certain intended advantages, even if they do not serve the active truth of human living. In their willing scramble for survival, people also readily finish each other off. Dividedness then rules human relationships. As existence devastates and wears out people's lives, it also drains them of vibrancy and generosity. In point of fact, as the culture of hypocrisy spreads, people's genuine desires become distorted, misrepresented, and suppressed. The lordship complex in the human scene further spurs serious cases of paranoia, neurosis, and viciousness.

ROMANS 2:1–11: THE RIGHTEOUS JUDGMENT OF GOD

Romans 2:1–11 exemplifies a further way of living as a family of God. This reading reflects on the way people can become judgmental of one another and hence fail to live according to the spirit of God's family. The momentum of this reading depicts well the spirit of judmentalism that makes it difficult to celebrate our identities as brothers and sisters of the same quality or as sons and daughters of God's family.

Ordinarily, one of our most difficult tasks of living pertains to coming to terms with our humanity. While we find ourselves enthused with the spark of divinity, we also find that we remain flawed and imperfect beings. The mystery of our humanity involves our being in a profound variety of ways. Our own struggles with human frailty, foibles, weakness, fragility, and the lapses of our rationality constitute concrete pathways to understanding our humanity. Understanding our own limitations and shortcomings needs to lead us to comparable consideration of others. Just as much as we struggle, other people struggle. Humility in the face of our own and other people's failings reflects a positive hallmark of our humanity come of age. Reflecting such humility in the lived experience of our interactive and interpretative world can be arduous. However, it remains worthwhile for us to always strive for such humility. In short, human frailties and attachments can play vital roles in the transforming experience of making us become more fully Christian.

In the letter to the Romans, St. Paul challenges the disconnect that happens when people live lives out of tune with their humanity. When we do not pay attention to and own up to the fragility of our humanity, we easily come to *demand* of others what we cannot do ourselves. As a result, in Romans 2:1–11, Paul confronts the common tendency to judge and condemn others. Such an attitude arises from a lack of humility before personal shortfalls and from lack of compassion when we encounter failings in others. Paul states, "Therefore you have no excuse, whoever you are, when you judge others; for in passing judgment on another you condemn yourself, because you, the judge, are doing the very same things" (Rom 2:1). Paul takes the experience or phenomenon of judging others quite seriously: "Do you imagine, whoever you are, that when you judge those who do such things and yet do them yourself, you will escape the judgment of God?" (Rom 2:3). Here Paul wants to make the point that when we throw dirt onto others, some of the dirt remains in our hands. Only through continual self-examination and change of heart can we abandon the ruinous judgmentalism that also undermines the flowering of our humanity and relationships.

Questioningly, Paul suggests: "Or do you despise the riches of his kindness and forbearance and patience? Do you not realize that God's kindness is meant to lead you to repentance?" (Rom 2:4) At the same time, we need to note that only God can change the human heart. God desires that we convert and change our hearts and lives in order to celebrate the experience and beauty of human familyhood. Negative energy means nothing less than this: that a certain unpleasant taste characterizes a judgmental personality. A judgmental person does not positively reach out to accommodate the other; he or she does not care enough to have a courteous talk with or understanding of the other. But God effects a turn away from judgmentalism only in collaboration with our willingness, desire, and freedom. On the whole, he brings positive changes in our lives if we so desire and cooperate with him. In fact, a heroic feat does not coincide with the experience and itinerary of our human conversion. In short, it does not lie within our power to bring about our own liberative transformation.

When we judge and condemn others, the attendant self-righteousness tends to involve or imply self-deception as a game we play with ourselves. When we deceive ourselves regarding our faults, we end up becoming blind to them. In the circumstances, the attitude or posture of criticizing others tends to go hand in hand with self-excuse for one's own shortcomings, weaknesses, or failures. This partially explains why Jesus, in his many encounters, attacked the Pharisees precisely for their duplicity. Jesus observed that the Pharisees loaded others with heavy burdens, which they themselves would not help to lighten (Luke 11:46). In other words, Jesus frequently noted how the Pharisees oftentimes failed to put themselves in the place of others, especially in their struggles or difficult moments. Their disjointed ideal for humanity required different standards for different people. When people act and live with double standards, they do so with contradictions and hypocritically. Such a trajectory of human behaviour often arises from negative pride, selfishness, prejudice, greed, favouritism, ignorance, and violence of the heart.

We do well to get in touch with our humanity because in that experience of presence to the self, we become able to connect with others compassionately. Then we can experience the exuberance of life in all its struggles, moorings, raptures, and the joyful interdependence of loving that makes all living worthwhile. God's intention for us cannot be less than this. In fact, when individuals embody with their words and actions the self-righteous, self-deceived, condemning judgment we can feel visceral disgust and anger, followed quickly by an immobilizing fear. At the same time this sensibility can be tempered by a simultaneous realization that we, human beings in our brokenness, can inadvertently harm another through our own ignorant reactive judgments. This remains especially so in relation to the disconnection and psychological carnage that our misguided acts can inflict on others.

What is more, in the moment of confrontation with judgmentalism, we easily experience an inability to hold the immensity of reconciling compassion in our thoughts, words, and actions. For we instinctively adopt the very dynamics of blaming and the punishing dynamic that we precisely abhor in judgmentalism. Of course, we must not forget that all judmentalism tends to bring with it some hubristic, poisonous, and whiney attitudes that make productive and meaningful relationships among people difficult to realize and celebrate.

But on a positive note, growing in understanding and awareness can transfigure the discomfort that we feel in the presence of self-deceived, self-righteous judgmentalism. And in the experiential moment of authentic self-presence, which coextends with divine presence, we become a part of the solution rather than a part of the problem of existence (i.e., that by which we know how we are). We live in the light. Then the signature marks of luminous presence feeds our existence with patience, gentleness, forgiveness, and compassion.

In consequence, reflection remains vital to growth in this life since only after we know how to bring out the best in ourselves can we bring out the best in others. Through reflection we acknowledge and accept our own vulnerability and learn how much we depend on generous and genuine people in our community. In fact, as we grow in our openness about our faults we embrace, as it were, the last frontier of honesty. Appropriating the awareness of our own lived discordance needs to help us be in touch with our humanity sensitively and compassionately.

Within this perspective, too, we must also immediately grant that by embracing and sharing with the most fragile in our world we truly gain the ability to articulate our own helplessness and dependence in existence, which reveal to us that ultimately we remain loved and must not live in anguish. We must know that the self, in all its beauty and ambiguity, lies at the root of liberative understanding and harnessing of our humanity.

Thus, in order to develop a dynamic and mature sense of self, we must appreciate strong familial bonds we have with other people, but we must make individual choices for this option before we can extend it outwardly relationally. Only then can we, together with others, truly experience and live life with zest and passion for the joy of living.

Nonetheless, it always takes and demonstrates personal selflessness to admit one's own mistakes. When people cannot accept their own mistakes they cannot easily uphold and respect the interests of others. When people admit their own mistakes they free themselves from vested interests for the sake of wholesome peace and coexistence. People choose hope over fear when they acknowledge and own up to their own mistakes and shadows. They also herald the promise of unity over dividedness. In the search for an experience and expression of oneness with others, people need to learn to free themselves from the urge to always be right so that they act with a sense of righteousness (which means being just, true, honest, charitable, and courageous).

Christian witness demands pastoral outreach and interior discipline as well as a balance between creativity and solitude as a way of expressing the work of the Spirit in our lives. It also implies flexibility, fluidity, and sharing in daily tasks and encounters. All this means that, one way or the other, Christian discipleship involves elements of personal attitudes of opening, widening, deepening, and integrating our lives with the ambiguous experience of being in a problematic world. After all, God shapes us with beliefs, interior motions, and attitudes founded on the truth of being human in this world. Moreover, we need to become vulnerable in order for God to build his kingdom within and among us. God nourishes us through the experiences and support we get from others and personal experiences by means of which we appropriate the richness of Christian heritage, the word of the scriptures, and the community in which we irrevocably pitch ourselves.

For those of us in ministry and positions of authority it becomes very important that we continually remain humble in the face of our own weaknesses and compassionate before the limitations of others. Furthermore, the practice of humility and compassion requires vigilance and consciousness for their continual renewal, efficacy, and assurance. Within this framework, it may also be recognized that some facets of life enable us to grow in this awareness. The forthcoming sub-sections consider and discuss the facets of being, understanding, and intervention.

Way of Being

Our way of being brings to mind how we present ourselves to or find ourselves before others, especially those who come to us for help. Our way of being refers to the visage of our self-presentation—who we are and how we are impact others. In this regard, fresh and radiant self-presentation constitutes an art that renews people's lives. When we present ourselves to others with sympathy and sensitivity, we understand them well. In this regard, it helps to ask the following guiding questions: Does our self-presentation offer others a sense of acceptance and a feeling of being at home with us? Does the way we show or reveal ourselves to them give them some peace and joy? In other words, how does our degree of sensitivity affect others with whom we interact?

The poor, the oppressed, the marginalized, and those who have suffered much at the hands of others can be very sensitive. This means that they can keep a careful distance from other people in spite of their immense desire for closeness. Frequently, such people have a keen intuition of dangerous relationships. They survive because they can foresee rejection, abandonment, weakness, and failure and forestall problems. Unfortunately, our way of being with others may remind them of past hurts and abuse. In these circumstances, we can cultivate an awareness of others' responses to us. Our body language and non-verbal communication may unwittingly make others fear becoming subjects of what they may perceive as yet another occasion of hurt and oppression. At the same time, the mental and emotional lives of the disadvantaged and people in need can easily become paralyzed when they realize that other people take them for granted. A nonjudmental way of being tends to engender trust, peace, and joy, which provide a spiritual climate of victorious love. Of course, people do experience more than they grasp so that the construction of meaning often comes with contexts and honed sensitivities. So, it always helps to re-create meaning for a struggling people through a positive way of being, expressible in variety of ways.

Way of Understanding

When people come to us with their issues, problems, or fears, what attitudes and approaches do they evoke within us and how do we express ourselves? Could it be that we tend to deal with such people of utmost vulnerability as mere cases of problems set before us in need of solutions?

Do we see such people as cases for daily dispensation of compassion in the way that we dispense doses of medication? Do we take the street kid for just a non-conforming miscreant? Do we see the parishioner who demands blessing as nothing but obsessed? Do we see the police officer as just another persecutor of the people? Paul, in Romans 2:1–11, challenges us not to judge and condemn others.

The way we understand other people's experiences and lifestyles molds our approaches and attitudes toward them. We can be judgemental and condemning or nonjudgmental and accepting. In his own life biography, as recorded in the gospels, Jesus demonstrated a way of understanding others in ways that accept and communicate compassion. In other words, how we deal and relate with, for example, people in detention, people suffering from HIV or AIDS, drug addicts, prisoners, alcoholics, prostitutes, the handicapped, the unemployed, and the homeless can be very revealing of the way we understand them. Our attitudes can, in fact, re-alienate and re-victimize such people who remain disadvantaged by their special circumstances of ill-health, discrimination, misfortune, or incapacity. Of course, over-skill in our responses can also easily bring a sense of crass opportunism, something we can always minimize, if not avoid altogether. And we do well to always remember that the internal fabric of life frequently tends toward the lowest energy point of the living organism—powerlessness or death.

Way of Intervening

When faced with the suffering humanity of others, how can we intervene in a helpful manner? What kind of intervention do we bring to light and attention? A positive intervention includes attitudes and language that bring forth acceptance, understanding, renewed life, and an atmosphere of protection, security, warmth, and love. Conversely, a negative intervention frequently engenders disappointments, frustrations, malice, insecurity, fear, and self-preoccupations with possessions. A helpful intervention in the lives of others requires some acknowledgement of our own limitedness in terms of inner and outward resources. At any rate, we variously remain forever caught up with the realities of greed, jealousy, frivolity, lust, resentment, violence of the heart, and lived insecurity.

Admitting our own limitations implies further that we all participate in the multiple drama and forms of human brokenness. This also means that we do more harm when we promise people more than we can offer or things beyond our own resourcefulness that can make us delve into hypocrisy. Humility requires that we acknowledge that we can assist where possible or necessary. At times this signifies that we assist in a limited way. A compassionate intervention sometimes means recognizing that we cannot or do not know how to help people in a given circumstance. To say or act otherwise would simply imply euphoric indulgence. Evidently, there can be such pressures in Church situations that demand immediate answers and solutions. However, people who know their limits and shortcomings and appreciate the weight of the problems or issues before them know when to intervene appropriately or whether they have requisite resources for effective intervention. Admirable and loving intervention always brings about new direction, meaning, self-knowledge, and a life of care and service.

Broadly speaking, the painful and grim reality of malice, wickedness, and woundedness exists in many people's lives. As the scourge of viciousness marks human relations, mistrust, suspicion, and antagonism become staples of personal and shared lives. Moreover, the ambiguity of personal, communal, and collective existence often means that we please and displease, impress and confound, and unite and divide. This ambiguity also implies that many individual and shared upheavals mar the paths of many people. At the same time, wounded and disappointed people aspire to and deserve peace, order, and stability. Christian righteousness, compassion, and healing can nurture, promise, and offer these needed experiences and realities.

So, it remains very important that we constantly examine ourselves regarding our way of being, understanding, and intervening into the life situations of others. We can have an unpleasant way of being, a poor way of understanding, and an unhelpful way of intervening in relation to situations of the human predicament. Everybody has shortcomings or faults. Finitude and contingencies mark *who and how we are*. In Romans 2:1–11, Paul challenges us to be nonjudgmental in our ways of being, understanding, and intervening in life. It remains un-Christian and contrary to the spirit of the Church as family not to exercise justice and the love of God in our ways of being, understanding, and intervening in life and existence. If we do not pay due attention, we risk exercising double standards. Christian discipleship means that our ways of relating with others bring them to their own desirability and beauty as persons, certainly without ignoring their flaws as human beings. In any case, in providing needed aid and compassion to people who come our way, we show concern and offer a human face of affirmation and respect. As followers of Christ, this act demands that we go well beyond the call of duty to active demonstration of generous spirit, understanding, care, and fellow-feeling. We always remain more similar than different from one another, despite differences, fears, and misunderstanding.

CONCLUSION

We must not sell human beings as we would do with items meant for commerce. We act wrongly when we turn people into merchandise. Human beings do not carry worth for commercial exchanges. Our incommensurable lovableness as persons cannot be earned. It symbolizes God's gratuity that comes with who we are as persons. The glory of humanity truly consists in making God, Jesus Christ, others, and the self known in positive light. In other words, our glory truly consists in building up the family of God. We can make this family lovable, beautiful, and celebrated through discerning charity and warm-heartedness, which resonate with and unveil the unconditional desirability, attractiveness, and lovableness of all.

Spreading the kingdom of God by building up the family of God also touches on the elements of trust, faith, hope, and charity present in us all. In other words, aspects of mystery exist in us and in all our relationships. When we blur the mysterious dimensions of our lives, we easily disrespect and abuse the beauty of human connections, interactions, and relationships. We become defensive and aggressive in our self-affirmations so that we scatter human communities and harm others. When we cannot celebrate the gift of each other as brothers and sisters of the same quality, we perfect the art of pettiness, viciousness, and malice as vehicles through which we stifle and destroy one another. God intends nothing but the best for each one of us. God intends not just life but also life in its fullness (John 3:16). He intends not just joy but also complete joy so that it makes us complete as human beings. This further implies participation and being caught up in the very struggle against what makes the full life not possible to many. We can always bring forth into this world extraordinary blessings and enlivening energies of life.

When we act like brothers and sisters of the same quality, we take care of one another and hold the family of God together. In other words, when we refuse to associate ourselves with our brothers and sisters, we begin to place ourselves outside God's family. We break the family bond, spirit, and warmth. God cares that we accept each other and stand together in celebrating the joy of living as one family.

If need be, God always waits for us to come together again. In fact, as we come close to God, we also grow in our responsibility for others and ourselves. Closeness and intimacy with God nourish and expand our sense of self-responsibility and responsibility toward others and life. When we experience God's graciousness and mercy, we become filled with love and tenderness for others and ourselves. Where people meet and come together with a true sense of human gifts, beauty, and identity, people truly worship and glorify God. Consequently, God delights and peace comes to our world. In this way, God's parenthood cannot be separated from a profound experience of liberation within the human community where people celebrate together the joy of living with refreshing warmth and care. Such a celebration embodies and heralds the good news.

In the last analysis, it remains important that we feel for others, offer them new sources of life, and invite them to become like our compassionate and loving God. Yet this must be done in a nonsentimental and realistic way. The message of the gospels challenges us to become sources of real life in the real world. In other words, we need to dare to stretch out our hearts and goodwill in blessing, welcoming, and being grateful for the gift of others in our lives. This outreach can be done joyfully and compassionately amidst the nitty-gritty issues of life. While selfless outgoingness makes demands on us, it also personally fulfils and positively influences common life and compassionately frees people for fruitful interactions and life with others. And we cannot talk meaningfully about human interactions without attention to the emotional aspect of life, a subject with which the next chapter deals.

6

Toward Functionally Healthy Relationships

INTRODUCTION

The upcoming considerations in this chapter particularly derive their importance from the fact that Christianity has tended to remain more a religion of the head than of the heart. In effect, Christianity needs to become the religion of the heart as well as the head so that there will exist little gap between what believers proclaim and what they live out in their day-to-day interactions and lives.

The reality of dysfunctional interpersonal relationships mark many people's lives. Dysfunctional relationships work, but they hurt. Many people find themselves caught up in interpersonal relationships with emotionally and mentally unstable persons who are problematic. Such relationships then get messy, complicated, and vicious because of inattention to emotional signals. In other words, it behooves us to always pay attention to emotional signals that others give and the signals we send out to others within relationships, together with their possible corresponding meanings and perspectives, which always remain cultural in character.

Within this framework, the forthcoming considerations draw attention to pertinent issues connected with affective human behaviors. In short, alertness to our emotional life makes us aware of motivations (namely, reasons for acting), something that we can periodically clarify with particular experiences of life. And when we become aware of and expand the knowledge of our motivations, we can respond to life honestly and generously, which also shapes the quality of our lives and relationships. Last but not least, in this chapter it must be particularly noted that emotions and feelings carry the same meanings and thus are used interchangeably throughout.

ALERTNESS TO EMOTIONAL LIFE

To begin, feelings take place within human intentional relatedness to the world. We belong to the world. This fact also means that we have a commitment to intrinsic meanings. As we participate in a story of origins and purposes within a community of persons who engage us in this world, we intuitively appreciate things. We project values onto them. We then have a felt meaning. Our dispositional placement elicits responses of feelings as we strive to maintain or restore narrative coherence to our lives within the context of forces that affect our existence. Attention to emotional life, then, refers to mindfulness about our feelings.

In a crucial way, our feelings announce and verify our human subjectivity, centeredness, and interiority with regard to self-perception and perception of the environment. Feelings always remain consubstantial with who we are at any given moment. Feelings link us inwardly with our relative sense of security and insecurity within obtaining life situations. We experience self-truth through feelings. A sense of impinging or affirming reality connects closely with the reality of our feelings. In this way, feelings provide us with a sense of our relationship with our operative sense of self whose equilibrium has been touched. Within this perspective, feelings enjoy and derive their authority from the acting or deciding self. Human interiority enthrones feelings by investing them with the powers they hold.

Resourceful handling of emotions remains an important aspect and asset in all relational experiences. When we do not pick up the feelings of each other well, the resulting misconstrual can lead to harsh emotional reactions, unfair treatment, or manipulation. So it helps to talk about and express our feelings verbally, especially with friends. Of course, we must communicate our emotions properly; it behooves us to know and strive to act on our emotions only discerningly. In fact, we should not expect people to read our feelings before we own and know them ourselves. Effectively, the onus remains on us with regard to how we know and deal with our feelings. It helps to anticipate our own feelings. Our bodies do give out emotional signals. When we get in touch with our bodies, we can know what happens within us emotionally through, say, our breathing, sweating, heartbeat, neck muscles, stomach, and eyes. In short, we relate resourcefully when we become literate of our own and other people's feelings and motives toward us and life.

In addition, it remains important to understand others in terms of where they are and where they come from emotionally. We do this well when we ask others their opinions and reflect on their feelings (namely, guess what happens to a person emotionally). Through this process we confirm, or at least let the others know, that we know what might be happening to them emotionally. It is not enough to suspect what others feel and sit on our suspicions; it is important to take a risk by asking them questions about their feelings. In this way, we make informed guesses.

When we feel insecure, we also become very sensitive. We attain a high degree of sensitivity. At such moments, we also have a wide latitude to decide who we can and would like to become. In fact, as we feel an immediate sense of relational disconnect we simultaneously long for connectedness and knowledge of the other in a context of trust, which also enables us to become aware of the forces and counter-forces at play within us as we participate in the world. In this way, when we feel unstable we can become creative in a world that does not easily yield meaning to our lives. As we gather and bring back together elements of our fractured lives, of our relationships, and of meanings, we begin to enact wholeness to our humanity and in our world.

In this regard, it becomes very important to pay attention to the feelings of others. Feelings reveal what goes on inside people. When we overlook feelings, it could mean that ours has been a history that did not pay due or close attention to emotional needs. It could also mean that we have not been on the receiving end of the question of how we feel. When we ask how the other feels, we bring the other into the picture of what engages our attention and loyalty. We create an awareness that generates a relationship. When we draw people's awareness to their emotional needs, they can attend to them in resourceful and right ways. People need to acknowledge, recognize, and where possible, name the feelings they go through and which, perhaps, control their lives. Often questions or issues of appropriate boundaries, friendships, significant connections, and human touch arise as well. Boundaries mean putting limits to our desires, thoughts, and actions within the usual context of our relational contacts. And relationships tend to have ambiguous and changing boundaries as perspectives evolve and shift. Different relationships admit and accept different kinds of limits, flaws, and shifts. And sometimes when we cross boundaries we erase them. Recognizing this nexus always serves us well because it always remains a transgression to meet one's emotional needs at the expense of others. In order to avoid this trespass, we do well to act with emphatic care, patience, and self-monitoring. This step further implies a deep consideration of others as others; otherwise they become people we need for our own ends.

Besides, we cannot always meet the emotional needs of the other. The other does not need to rely on us as the answer to his or her emotional life. We cannot provide all the answers, nor should we become the focus of the life of the other. In effect, it becomes important to monitor other people's emotional responses to our persons. Of course, we can enjoy their company, share times with them, and be resourceful for them. But we must also be willing to back off and do something else outside our friendships and people close to us. This makes possible a healthy dynamic in our relationships. In the same vein, ethical responsibility within contexts of relationships then means that a person does not act on the emotional needs of the other. We do well not to feel too important in our relationships. Otherwise we engage in the making of a personality cult. In good relationships we can always share our gifts, reach out, and focus on what builds up life.

We also need to be sensitive to our own emotions and how others feel about us. Our feelings (which communicate our desires, inclinations, intentions, motivations, and tendencies) provide gateways to our inner lives, which constitute the reality that we live at a given moment. Armed with self-understanding and as occasions demand it, we can then respond responsibly and through explicit discussions about our relationships with our relational partners. This response may particularly express itself in terms of how we see the relationship and what inchoate expectations (namely, demands) our relational partners and we may harbor. When we pay attention to our emotional life and dynamics, we also learn to be careful in our language and behaviors and the consequences that they can carry. We can accordingly regulate our friendship barometers. When we fail to pay close attention to the feelings of others, they can attack us out of frustration, disappointment, and expectations that we unwittingly generate and do not meet. Even the question or issue of telling the truth about everything to everyone can be harmful if we do not pay attention to how truth-telling affects oneself and the other. The mental and emotional maturity of the other must carry some weight in every disclosure of the truth. What others feel does matter. When others come to us, they do not come to a neutral ground; they come with pre-understanding, prejudices, perceptions, and expectations about us.

Notably, then, we need to appreciate that our expectations position us in relation to our future situations, and that position affects our procedures and decisions about life as well as our sense of control and manipulation of situations. In this sense, the stake of our expectations directs our lives and affects our grasp of specifics and details within a relationship.

When things begin to go wrong in a relationship, it helps to try to retrace our steps in order to identify and understand where the relationship went wrong or went off track or simply changed. We can do this through recollection, re-examination of consciousness, and reaching out to wise or professional people whose company and skills can awaken us to new realities about ourselves and our relationships. In this way, we face suffering or difficulties meaningfully so that new life arises from the crushed and broken aspects of our lives. We then can embark on the pathway of experiencing, appropriating, and cultivating anew the freedom of love and communion. With every relational difficulty or any form of suffering, we can become imbued with new emotional awareness and strength, which then pervade our spirit and orientation in life with freshness and creativity.

In a conflict situation, it often helps to review and re-evaluate our expectations and reset our goals. After all, the crucible of experience always tests and verifies the realistic, creative, and productive character of our expectations. In this regard, it becomes important to recognize the utmost importance of discerning that we do not just take anybody on board relationally. Interestingly yet indicatively, people with little self-respect and poor self-image can respond to us out of compunction. In the process they fail to act and achieve healthy expressions or postures of wholeness. When we do not meet or satisfy their emotional expectations, they can make unscrupulous attempts to slander us in some of the most disconcerting and perhaps also twisted ways. In short, people frequently take options on the basis of built-up anger (i.e., the frustration of expectations) and pain because they feel hurt and deprived somewhere or somehow and cannot cope in a healthy way with their emotional frustrations. This is also to say that as people fail to take control over their feelings, their feelings take control of them.

No matter how enthusiastic, exciting, and affirming the prospects may present themselves, when it comes to forming new interpersonal relationships we should not easily take people on board. We need to watch out for signals of emotional or mental instability or an unstable life. This further requires that we become aware of our own feelings, needs, and space; for people can easily work on our own feelings and needs and take advantage of them. In view of the fact that so many people look for love and attention, we always need to make decisions about our own need for attention and affection according to our state of life. Affection normally makes us feel cared for, safe, and close to one another. Through affection we join our feelings of love and desire. "I like being with So-and-So" typically expresses people's affection for one another. It simply means that they care for the emotional needs and wants of one another. At this point, people also normally begin to take special care of their self-presentation and decorum: physique, dress, personal ambiance, and overall appearance.

Many people live broken and scattered lives, and they remain constantly on the lookout for someone to hold them together. In effect, it always helps when we remain mindful of boundaries within relationships so that we do not go where we do not need to go. Boundaries within relationships set limits to what we can and cannot do according to our chosen states of life. Limiting oneself to set boundaries or standards with regard to thoughts, words, and interactions always offers protection from hurtful misunderstandings and destructive intent of others.

It is of value to note that we should not take emotional communication for granted. A lot of such communication takes place as people relate with one another. If we do not read and listen to emotional reality within relationships we easily make blunders in our relationships with others. After all, nonverbal communication constitutes our most primitive way of connecting with others. When we lack the ability to decipher and understand such communication, we become socially inept. The key lies in alertness and attention to comments, suggestive thoughts, slips of the tongue, bodily expressions, and flippancies. Unless we understand the clues to the language of primitive communication, we risk distorting our relationship with others. We further risk transferring to others our narrow modes of relating that we experienced and learnt in our upbringing. As a result, we fail to acknowledge, recognize, and appropriate our desires, interests, and expectations resourcefully. In the process, we also fail to appropriately meet or satisfy these realities in others. They can then become disappointed and angry with us. Of course, we need to bear in mind the fact that at times labels with which people come to us simply cover up defenses that can collapse in the context of emotional warmth.

When we internalize and become aware of the emotional needs of others and our expectations within the context of relationships, we free ourselves from the risks of inordinate attachments or clinging attitudes. The clinging tendency that typifies emotional attachments easily leads to warped perceptions, disorientation, and misrepresentations of lived realities of life. These distortions often blind us about motivations that control or direct our lives or the lives of others. Under these circumstances, we cannot normally make informed and responsible decisions that become life-giving, individually and interpersonally.

EMOTIONS, SEXUALITY, AND HUMAN GROWTH

As noted already, within relationships people can come to us with labels. The initial impressions of these labels can make us naïve about the development of relationships between such people and ourselves. Oftentimes, however, such labels also represent defense mechanisms people devise in order to cope with some of their life experiences. Labels can mask discomfort and insecurity, which touches on and devours the lives of people in very personal and deep ways. People who primarily mark themselves with labels may need supplementary meaning to transcend their experience of vulnerability and fragility. Undoubtedly, labels with which people identify can collapse in the face of emotional needs or demands. In the circumstances, an upsurge of attitudes easily results. Initially, it can be exciting and could appear exceptional that some people come to us. But such attitudes toward others who come into our lives may, in fact, reflect a lack of problematic experience in our relational past or a facile logic of heroism in life that arises from inexperience. Indiscretion that comes with inexperience frequently means that we have not grown and discovered certain emotional sensibilities beyond immediate reflexes. When we remain unaware of the existential meanings of labels people carry with them, we easily find ourselves in a relational context that constantly seeks and demands affective compensation from us. Subsequently, when we cannot sustain, care for, and make such a relationship grow, we risk abandoning or giving up on the relationship. As a result, some very negative consequences on our personal and social existence may result from acts that proceed from inflamed passions. Blows from an emotionally frustrated, thwarted, or disappointed person can devastate everything in minutes.

Observably, too, emotions take place within a context of our sense of maleness and femaleness, which refers to our sexuality. In fact, our sexuality virtually coincides with or relates very closely to our sense of self. As a characteristic of human existence, sexuality concerns and reaches to the innermost core of a person. It involves the whole person. Sexuality characterizes us at physical, psychological, and spiritual levels. At the same time, sexuality exposes our incompleteness. It reveals our deep human need for another. The fact of being male or female reveals and expresses our need and demand for the complementary other who can complete us in a certain sense, at least relationally. Within this framework, our sexuality urges us toward recognition, love, friendship, and communion of freedom in human togetherness. Acceptance, affirmation, care, and unity of persons belong to the rich purpose of sexuality. As a way of openness and relating to and fruitful communication with another, our sexuality constantly refers us to the fruitful qualities of self-possession and awareness. Indeed, we talk of the union of the sexes in contexts of interpersonal coming together, of attachments, and of openness to the gift and nourishment of life. Above all, people most deeply desire and yearn for the experience of vulnerability and surrender within interpersonal relationships.

Here, we may point out that it is not always easy to become vulnerable to anybody. It takes courage, determination, and dependability to be open and vulnerable to another. In fact, strength of personality does not negate sensitivity and tenderness. Self-accepting persons know that they lose nothing by being vulnerable. When people speak and express themselves and their views and expectations to others, they help the others know where they are in relation to things and situations that they refuse to be indifferent to or refuse take for granted.

The fact remains that the bottom line of human interpersonal relationships and togetherness seems to consist in the struggle of discerning trust. We want to trust enough in life so that we may show our weaknesses to another. Trust molds our attitudes and behaviors. As a result, we deeply yearn for vulnerability and surrender emotionally, psychologically, and even sexually. We seem unable to make ourselves whole outside the trusting contexts of human relationships.

At this point, we may note unequivocally that the fact of maleness and femaleness extends to all human beings and in a noncontingent (i.e., inherent) way. Our sexuality relates to our humanity in a much more profound way than our requests, pleas, and petitions do. Urgently and peremptorily, we remain male or female irrespective of our race, skin color, religious affiliation, nationality, property qualification, marital status, or gender. As a result, we insist upon our sexuality without embarrassment or shame. No amount of love or compassion substitutes for our sexuality. Sexual differences between human beings exist and remain relevant facts of life that mark our personal identities. Every human being retains sexual significance that precedes social constructions of boundaries in human relations. Sexual differences and directedness institute respect and constraints in human behaviors. In addition, they reflect and motivate the underlying human urge for wholesome sexual complementarity. In other words, the marvelous inscription of human sexuality serves the recognitional function by indicating reaction-constraining awareness, forethought, and autonomy within relationships. Our sexuality enables us to grow in responsible human self-mastery.

Each human's sexuality exists in a reciprocal relationship to others. Basic communicative design and aspects for unity, complementarity, and sexual diversity mark the human fact of being in the world as male or female. Thus, the working out of the meaning of human sexuality that endows us with wholesome personal love always remains a significant aspect of purposeful living. We do justice to the body when we appropriately direct it toward purposes consistent with its inbuilt natural wisdom. In short, the experience of our sexuality relaxes and fulfills us when it remains wholesome in terms of bodily function and design.

Emotionally, people yearn for meaning and deep peace that comes from the practice of sexual sanity and fidelity. In other words, our sexual choices should make us admirable and authentic people committed in wholesome love. This is also to say that more exists to life than pleasure, possessions, and power. In this regard, too, as we work through the abiding sense of our own sexuality, community life can provide needed support and a sense of relational validation. Of course, we must not lose sight of the fact that our sexuality does not set all the terms for who and what we become as persons. In fact, relationships do make up an enormous part of the totality of our lives.

NEW BIRTH

Recollection and Emotional Depth

Without a doubt, God created our sexuality for a reason: it urges us outward toward others. We repeatedly experience the need for others in our lives. As a man or woman, we each draw people to ourselves emotionally. Some of these people seek to seize us. In reaching out to others, our sexuality enables us to make impact on others. And it becomes important to reflect enough on the impact we make on people who relate with us. The impact we make on others who relate with us matters. Of course, our impact on others remain largely experiential (i.e., intellectual and emotional). As we engage people, we impact them. Consequently, we do well to take time and look back to see what impressions and impacts we make on others, either as men or women. All this demands our willing acceptance and recognition that feelings rule human relationships. We need to become aware of the emotional experience that underlies and forms every relationship. We do this well and resourcefully through recollection, by means of which we also energize ourselves for life-giving relationships.

Recollection requires separation from the ordinary circumstances of life so that one becomes a subject of discernment, namely open to understanding and receiving the life-giving Spirit of God. Or again, recollection requires that we distance ourselves from noise, distractions, and crowds. Such a distance offers us some sense of personal space and an anchor by means of which we can attain clarity, simplicity, and spontaneity with respect to the sense of our own persons. We gain interior access to and learn the priority of being over having. The experience rekindles our sense of self with freshness, creativity, and freedom, which then make us better and more fulfilled persons. The resulting wisdom, sensitivity, and sense of virtue that recollection ushers in enable us to modify and create experiences that assert the ascendancy and triumph of life in our problematic world.

Through recollection[1] we access levels and thresholds of our own consciousness through the act of earthly presence and centeredness. Recollection connects and binds us with our being, the ground and basis of our interior fullness that coincides with the truth of our persons. In being, we connect with our spiritual instinct and our inner truth as the spiritual realities of our lives that invite our own selfhood and most original

---

1. In this work, recollection, ingatheredness, and contemplation remain interchangeable terms with the same meaning.

potentialities. Our being explains why we want and desire satisfaction at a deep level of living, which does not equal what others ordinarily expect of us. As that which allows us to be most at home with ourselves, our being grounds our generosity in service to others. It also enables us to aspire to and live fully our dreams.

In point of fact, being means that we have the power of presence within us as something created with us that seeks to come out and reach fulfillment. Of course, presence of being remains always deliberate and voluntary. As a potential characteristic, many issues hinder our presence from maturing or reaching full expression. This signifies also that as human beings we frequently encounter issues that hinder the development of love and our capacity to love. In other words, rarely do we have powerful and rewarding opportunities that enable us to learn from, deal with, and grow through issues lovingly.

What is more, being further implies that by nature people need each other. Our need for each other comes in many forms: brother, sister, friend, neighbor, and the stranger. As a result, we find that often many people get better through, say, gossip. So, our being impacts other people. We have the power of presence by means of which we influence our surroundings. Our presence impacts and influences our contexts or environment; we affect what exists around us. Every human being has that which pulls people toward him or her. Our impact on another or our environment often happens without our awareness.

Moreover, being coincides with the pre-deliberative tie that links people with one another. By nature we look for presence of the other for support through our various experiences, thoughts, and behaviors. When we access presence, we feel and get better as persons. Presence enables people to identify and understand their own core issues or what goes on in their lives. The resulting relational assurance and experience then heal and comfort them as they also begin to see realities and things differently. In short, presence protects us against the experience of feeling lost, forgotten, or neglected spiritually.

Our availability as persons then remains always a key ingredient to our existence. The power of being attracts people to us; our being moves others toward our persons. When we allow others to access our presence, the energy of our being, we offer our given source of human support to them.

Furthermore, the experience of being, inseparable from living truth, makes us aware of our inner integrity and deep interior harmony that sustain us with a capacity for peacefulness. In this way, we meet and encounter our life, which we then explore, transform, and celebrate. We recall and enter into the sacred space, the pulse of our persons, and the energy of our relationships. As we gain a deep awareness of our life and way of being, interior peace becomes accessible and available through presence. Thus, our human ingatheredness coincides with being inside our daily experiences that the gift of centered presence mediates and authenticates. The illuminating light of being touches and grasps us. As we come to glimpse and experience the fullness toward which our life flows, we see and re-access our existence in new and welcoming ways.

Being means that our creation as persons remains a gift we bring to this life. We did not choose to be the persons we are. Even our parents did not choose who we would be. In a sense, then, we had absolutely no role with regard to who we are as persons. Accordingly, our being means that we accept the gift of our life and existence from the tomb to the womb. It also implies accepting all of our life's demands, needs, expectations, and personal interdependence. Coexistence with others further implies that we can never become completely autonomous beings. In effect, we have an incomplete gift of integrity of our persons so that initiative, discipline, and responsibility cannot be separated from personal life in this world.

Or again, in being we acknowledge and accept the particular, unique, and unrepeatable person that we symbolize. This also means, however, that we delight in the wonder, resplendence, and mystery of our persons with all the physical inadequacies, psychological habits, and spiritual betrayals. Moreover, God remains the ground of our being. Divine excellence radiates and overflows our lives with light, love, and hope. So, in God we receive our unconditional affirmation and celebration of ourselves. Through being we accept, love, and honor ourselves.

But we cannot completely root ourselves in our being because of interior and external forces of dissipations. Frequently, our social and interactive worlds tell us that our acceptance and worth as persons come with what we wear, things we possess, beverages we drink, vehicles we drive, or with acting and believing in only certain ways. In other words, media of extrinsic validation put on us an enormous pressure by making us dependent on the acceptance and approval of others for our self-confidence, self-worth, and personal assurance. Furthermore, because of our pervasive conditional sense of self, envy, jealousy, populism, and covetousness constitute the staples of our ordinary, day-to-day existence. Yet we commonly compare our total selves with only the external selves of the others we see.

In recollection, then, we come with openness, bringing with us our strengths and weaknesses, urges and hopes, past and present. In this way, we bring the real being we are, not a straw man, or straw woman for that matter, for illumination by our interior rhythms. In this way, we bring ourselves to the transcendent power of life and allow it to penetrate our whole psychological life. In the process, we savor and nourish a mysterious understanding of our person. We touch on the exultant joy of life as we apprehend the experience of interior freedom and harmony. Subsequently, an extraordinary presentiment fills and opens us up to a luminous source that suffuses our world. The experience then flowers in our activity, occupations, creativity, and solitude. The world becomes a marvelous and abundant field of activity and fulfillment.

In the end, recollection enables new roots of joyful life and quieting wisdom to spring forth in our lives. When our emotional life springs from such awareness, we become sensitive to and respect other people's sensitivities and desires. The innate force of recollection centers us on the plenitudinous plane, a felt reality within that releases us to ourselves. The plane of recollection spontaneously frees us from our self-preoccupying selves. We rediscover the sense of life's intrinsic significance. This discovery changes the way we approach others and how we readily say things that become significant to them. In this way, we heighten our emotional alertness and perceptiveness as wellsprings of the extraordinary that inspire and nurture enthusiasm for all relational life.

The foregoing considerations do not in any way detract or take us far afield from our subject of human sexuality. Admittedly, as recollected people we live our sexuality affirmatively and resourcefully. As an act of openness to living truth, recollection enables people to live their sexuality with lightsome dimensions and perspectives of meaning, love, and hope that overcome loneliness, emptiness, and the sense of uselessness. In this way, we come to honor, accept, and enjoy our evolving reality and spontaneous presence in this world.

NEW BIRTH

Harnessing Emotional Build Up in Relationships

We carry out the task of living as men and women. In other words, we cannot take our manhood or womanhood for granted. Our sexuality (i.e., our being male or female) provokes certain emotions in people around us. The more we offer others emotional security, the more we need to be in a state of emotional alertness (i.e., the more we need to be people who recollect). We cannot take the emotional relations of people toward us for granted. For if we understand and know what people relating with us look for, we can make wise decisions and not allow certain dynamics to develop. We can also help them deal with their emotional needs or demands resourcefully.

Notably, only a thin veil separates love and hate in relationships. Even angry people get attracted to us; their anger does not prevent or cancel our appeal to them. Nonetheless, we need to know that some people's anger arises from their rebellion toward their experiences and some truth about their persons. In the circumstances, such people can also experience much confusion. In other words, if we do not pay attention to the feelings of people who relate with us, we may miss important clues to their personalities and desires. Consequently, we can act on miscues. Yet if we fail to meet these people's emotional needs or demands, they can always fight back with a vengeance. This means that whenever we fail to be emotionally intelligent, we often cause a lot of hurt in the other who relates with us. In short, our talents and giftedness can become liabilities against us and against those close to us or against those who relate with us.

Tellingly, we can have enormous power over others. We can influence them deeply. But we need to reflect on the immense power we may have over other people around us. We can use this power to give life or to eviscerate others. We need to continually become conscious of how we use our ability to influence and affect people around us. The risk remains that we can spread ourselves thinly and carelessly. In the process, we also attract a lot of attention and gather a lot of nonsense around ourselves.

Of course, to enter any meaningful relationship, we need to trust ourselves. Every relationship remains, in principle, a risk. Paradoxically, a genuine friendship depends on who and how we are or how we present ourselves. The quality of friends we attract can reflect the kind of persons that we project, at times by mistake, at a given moment or context or the

148

compensation people can make out of us. But even more crucially, when we reach out to others genuinely and honestly, we also need to be cautious. In other words, in a context where the risk of developing a dysfunctional relationship remains real, we must not overdo relationships (i.e., developing too much communication or contact or getting together too frequently or substantially). Our other friends who know us can always tell us whether developing a particular relationship remains a good idea at all. In any case, we need to leave some space, a buffer zone, between our friends and ourselves. When relationships become too tight, they blind us. It helps to keep friends on the side and not in front or behind us. In this way, they cannot push or block us so that our goals and values remain clear. Or again, relationships do not exist to make others dependent on us nor we dependent on others. This means that for every relationship we need to have other friends and contexts of enlivenment so that we may spread out our relational energies.

When we become too strongly immersed in a relationship, withdrawal from such a relationship cannot but be hurtful to the other partner in the relationship. When we move away or when our friends do so, we can feel very empty. We experience a deep sense of loss. Relational separation can cause us a lot of anger and pain or the other person can hit back at us ferociously. Under these circumstances, a relationship can become nefarious and cruel. This means that closeness and distance need to exist together in every relationship. A balance of closeness and distance in a relationship helps safeguard against emotional suffocation. In a context where we realize that a relationship makes excessive demands on us, we need to become aware of it. This means also that we sit down with the other person with whom we relate and discuss matters candidly. Often assumptions, presuppositions, and expectations that shape motivation play out in relationships. Accordingly, we can put early brakes on certain elements and dynamics of our relationships. When we relate at different levels, we cannot help avoid ambiguity and confusion. Unless we regularly examine our relationships, double messages may color them with murkiness and ambiguity.

Furthermore, tensions must be expected where people relate. In a relationship tensions and conflicts often arise. At some point, people in a relationship disagree in belief or attitude. The attitudes the parties to a relationship adopt then become very important. In this regard, dialogical attitudes make possible a favorable outcome. Attitudes of bitterness and harshness do not console nor inspire understanding and reconciliation in a relationship. Where people interrupt and contradict each other, they cannot listen patiently to one another. They also cannot answer questions well or respond kindly and honestly. It then becomes increasingly difficult for such people to pardon frailties. Fondest expectations and lived hopes easily fade in the horizon of bitterness. In other words, tension in a relationship can offer friends opportunities to discuss differences. And when friends resolve conflicts amicably, they strengthen the relationship.

Men and women do not enter relationships with the same psychological setup. Unless we realize this fact, we risk our relationships with terrible conflicts. This also means that when we relate with the opposite sex it helps to pay attention to the other when we share something. We need to think of the impact of what we share on the other. It behooves us not to share information and facts carelessly. When we observe the body language and behavior of the other, which reveals a lot about the person, it can alert us to boundary issues or unspoken intentions. Keeping to our boundaries protects us in relationships. At times we may have to ask the other with whom we relate directly how what we do or say impacts him or her in terms of perceptions, ideas, feelings, or imagination.

When emotional depth develops, say, between two people, they make a lot of emotional savings into each other. They invest a lot of affection in the relationship. This investment affects them in a deep way. Partners to a relationship can then begin to want to own each other. The risk of possessiveness increases. That is also to say that the relationship easily devolves into something that one possesses. This explains the importance of clarity about expectations at the beginning of a relationship. Clarity helps both parties to know how much they can give one another and how far they can go with the relationship. If we, as parties to a relationship, do not clarify expectations, we risk developing different emotional expectations and attitudes. Actually, emotional expectations and demands frequently function within frameworks of individual perceptions shaped by developing and different histories and accompanying relational expectations. This fact also calls for some sensitivity to cultural and historical differences when relationships take place within intercultural contexts. Moreover, when attractions between two people in a relationship deepen, clarity about expectations can become murky, which also intensifies relational seductiveness. As a result, the risk of exceeding stated expectations increases as well.

Accordingly, as we enter into relationships with others, we need to become aware of their and our own emotional build up. We need to ask the question, "Does the other person feel and think the same or in a similar way as I do or vice versa?" Also, we must realize that when other people confide in us relationally, we become a treasure for them. We become a resource for them. We appeal to them in some very personal and special way. Simply put, we come to mean much to them; we make them feel significant as we give them much emotional validation. Tellingly, when we make another person with whom we relate feel emotionally at home with us, we risk making him or her dependent on or obsessive about us. Moreover, when someone wants to relate with us at the sexual level but we cannot respond favorably, we can cause so much anguish in him or her. In this regard, misunderstandings repeatedly arise in friendships between men and women due to unaddressed sexual tensions. These same difficulties may also exist in a relationship or friendship where persons belong to the same sex. Of course, other people's desires for us and our desires for them normally come about through experiences of, say, security, care, confidence, warmth, protection, charm, and love that we offer. These frameworks make people attractive and desirable. At the same time, they also offer the key to understanding fierce anger, pervading malice, and nefarious intentions that sometimes play out when relationships hit obstacles, begin to fall apart, or break up.

Responsibility and foresight require that in order to retool and address issues within relationships one can begin by removing distortions or illusions of false comfort that arise from the sense of being in a relationship. Sometimes we remain better off outside certain relationships because they drain us of energies for life. At times, this task of getting out of relational distortions requires that a person acts with immediacy and urgency in order to address tensions and imminent fallout in their relationships. And this needed response starts with and requires that we redefine or recalibrate our relational expectations, which normally enables us to develop a working frame for renewing and moving a relationship forward or in a new direction.

In fact, when we do not recognize, meet, cater for, or satisfy our emotional needs and demands, they often dictate their choices in our lives. They clamor for attention and expression. Frequently, such needs and demands express themselves through our careless longings for love, care, affirmation, acceptance, and friendship. Noticeably, we do bring different needs and demands with us when we enter into relationships with others. We often enter into relationships with others as adults or as children. This means that we bring different emotional needs and demands with us when we initiate or enter into a relationship with another person. Accordingly, we need to know and assume responsibility for our emotional needs and demands by becoming aware and taking care of them. In the end, alertness to our recurrent emotional states means that we take responsibility for them and the quality of our relationships with other people. This responsibility further involves continual awareness of what goes on within others and ourselves. It also entails making explicit decisions to live with the emotions within us. Furthermore, it signifies the process and decision to accept or not accept the other person in a context of reciprocity, mutuality, and complementarity in certain respects.

Taking care of our emotional needs and demands means getting in touch with movements within us so that we do not simply plough into and harm people through our behaviors or conduct. What we experience within comes out in our external relationships. Over and over again, it behooves us to constantly take care of our bodies and our psyches and identify our needs for, say, regular physical rest and relaxation.

EMOTIONAL CARE AND THE FAMILY OF GOD

As it stands, to have a sex or gender means to be cut off; namely, it signifies some incompleteness as a human being. This experience of not being whole, then, cannot be separated from basic human life. A man or woman in himself or herself lacks wholeness or wholesome harmony. Even when we become conscious of this fact, our consciousness does not cancel this experience that continually urges us toward complementary wholeness with and through others. On our own we remain incomplete as human persons. We cannot live a wholesome life without others. This fact makes us emotionally vulnerable to other people. Our meaning as persons demands and involves others who complement us. In effect, we become complete when others complement us.

In a sense, human completeness implies man and woman coming together. As a man, some elements of the woman always remain necessary and vice-versa. The primary issue concerns how far we may live and express human sexual complementarity. The difference depends on the choices we make in life. Whatever the case may be, we remain emotionally fragile or affectively vulnerable on our own. In essence, vulnerability comes with our need and demand for others. When we trust others and open ourselves to the liberality of their presence and experience we, in effect, make ourselves vulnerable to them. So, when we go to another in trust we make ourselves vulnerable to him or her. We experience and express emotional fragility as we entrust others with our felt insecurities. This also means, however, that we go to others with our emotional needs and demands. When we relate to and with others, we carry our emotional needs and demands with us. Life with others implies or touches on our need for their affection and support. We constantly carry with us the needs and demands for affection, love, acceptance, affirmation, guidance, and support.

We need to recognize and become aware of our own emotional needs and demands. This acknowledgment also refers us to our own shadows, weaknesses, and limitations. When we acknowledge and become conscious of our emotional needs and demands (an exercise we always need to carry out), we clarify much about issues that crop up in our relationships. Moreover, sexual needs center themselves around emotional life. So, we initiate the process of liberating ourselves from sexual carelessness and fragility when we become aware of our emotional needs, demands, and vulnerabilities.

When we fail to become aware of our own emotional needs and demands, we put ourselves in a potential relational trap. We fail to know how our emotional needs and demands put pressure on and affect our relationships. The risk always remains that we try to meet our emotional needs and demands in other people or spend our lives defending our vulnerability in others. We can spend a lot of our lives meeting our emotional needs and demands in other people. When we acknowledge our own needs, weaknesses, and vulnerability, we listen to and tame the unconscious dynamics that influence our lives and our relationships.

Acknowledging our own emotional needs, demands, and vulnerability constitutes the existential process of homecoming. We accept and make a home for them with our persons and personality. In the process, we also grant that accepting our strengths does not preclude embracing our personal weaknesses. And when we relate with another, we can listen to and recognize emotional resonances that go on between us. We understand and come to know what goes on between us when we relate with one another or certain individuals.

Emotional needs and demands frequently have to do with relating with others. When we become conscious of our emotional needs and demands, we can deliberately accommodate and go out of ourselves to meet other people's needs. We also practice the art of thinking and reflecting on our own emotional needs and demands, which often take on their own life out of consciousness, and therein lay their dangers. Our emotional needs and demands can drive us wild; they can make us mad. People can go to every length to meet their emotional needs and demands in us. In one sense, we cannot separate emotional health from our wellbeing. Certainly, we may feel embarrassed to acknowledge certain emotional needs and demands we experience. But it always liberates when we acknowledge honestly our affective needs and demands, at least to ourselves.

When we acknowledge our own emotional needs and demands, we also allow people to make mistakes. In the process, we do not necessarily feel overly strongly about issues. When we integrate our emotional needs and demands, as necessary dimensions of our persons, we also accept weakness, failure, rejection, and nonacceptance as parts of who we are. We fit and honor these realities as we own and appropriate them. Instead of constantly fighting them, we need to befriend our emotional needs and demands.

We should not judge our emotions. We only need to judge our actions. For example, the feeling of anger only tells us where we are with people, situations, and events. We do well to get in touch, for example, with our own emotional needs and demands for affection. People frequently come to us seeking it, and we regularly go to others seeking it. When we ignore our need and demand for affection, for example, and in the process throw others away, we hurt them or they hurt us if they abandon us. Then we or they can take revenge. In this respect, people can go to great lengths to remain in control. We need connection with our emotional needs and demands, especially those we particularly feel embarrassed about. If we do so, we can make our own decisions about them. And when we make decisions we need to think of the consequences of our actions, lest we become inhuman through thoughtless acts. Our emotional needs and demands offer us opportunities to get in touch with another side of ourselves that we do not frequently embrace and appropriate. Oftentimes we get in touch with what goes on in the depths of our being through our feelings.

Frequently, too, when we sort out our emotional needs and demands, which express themselves through feelings, we become aware of boundaries as well. We then make conscious decisions with regard to others. In this way, we learn how to act when a relational context offers us, for instance, much resistance. Often the natural tendency to rescue or protect other people can easily put us in a trap as well. We tend to respond to other people's own woundedness without much awareness. We must not be careless in how we respond to people's emotional needs and demands as we further leave a mark on them in the process. When we touch other people's lives, they want to associate with us. In our relationships we must avoid or minimize carelessness. This also implies a sense of self-responsibility that owns up to the totality of our persons. In other words, we can have a lot of power when we make emotional impacts on others, and this power can, in turn, hurt us if we do not harness it wisely. Significance and weight of our persons come with owning the totality of who we are: goodness, giftedness, needs, and careless tendencies.

We must not take people with whom we relate for granted. In other words, we must not live without awareness of how we impact them. This awareness means knowing how we get others involved with us and how we become involved with others relationally. But we do this well when we understand who we are and who we want to become. This further implies making conscious and deliberate decisions about who we are and reflectively expanding our knowledge of ourselves. In the process, we broaden our self-perceptions and with them, our self-definition and our availability to life itself.

When we attend to the details of our lives, we become alert to our own instincts, tendencies, and intuitions. As a result, we refuse to let circumstances dictate, drive, and define the directions of our lives. Rather, we consciously and reflectively make choices about our lives and attend to issues that mark and show up in our lives. Life, as it were, ceases to simply carry us along.

Accordingly, it remains important in relationships to ask ourselves some very important questions. Some such questions include: Why do people come into our lives? What do they want from us? Why would someone want to associate with us? Where does a given relationship seem to take us? We need to ask these questions because some people have very clear and definite intentions for coming into our lives. People do not come into our lives for decorative purposes. They do not participate in our lives ornamentally. Some people come to us looking for esteem and prestige, which they derive from associating with us. Others come to us looking for money, sex, or offspring, which they can later use to blackmail or ruin us, sometimes in vicious and malicious ways. Frequently, people do not divulge their intentions so that they can trick or trap us into a relationship that we may embrace with naiveté. When we enter a relationship innocently or simply out of trust, we risk a tumultuous and uncertain denouement or a shattering and nasty end. When we sort and clarify motives of people with whom we enter into relationships, we anticipate and take care of future mishaps and traps.

Encouraging questioning attitudes toward our relationships become even more urgent and necessary if we find ourselves in positions of influence or when we bubble with energy and remain accepting of others without being choosy. This same attitude applies when we find ourselves successful in life yet remain simple, straightforward, or unassuming in our relationships, despite, for instance, talents, wit, intelligence, and wealth.

Furthermore, alive and enthusiastic persons give others life. Heaviness or dark clouds rarely hang around such persons. Often such people radiate light and fire, as it were, as they enliven the world around them. In effect, exciting and enthusiastic people easily become centers of attraction, especially if they also show sensitivity and protection to people toward whom they relate. Such people need to develop the habit of asking for space and time before they respond to requests and demands others make on or direct at them. In this way, they give themselves the chance to discern well how to respond in ways that make profitable use of their positive energies. Moreover, every time a person brings emotions and reason together, something that requires some reflective time and space, when it comes to decision-making, that person tends to act resourcefully. The risk always remains that people do allow their feelings to decide the course of their actions so that they risk falling with a thud, especially if their lives carry much stake. When reason and emotions coexist in a healthy way, we can articulate and embody the virtues of piety, courage, temperance, and justice in our relational sense. Frequently, a given context provides the tone and approaches on how best to negotiate and relate reason and emotions in our lives.

We act recklessly when we do not take time to reflect on possible costs and consequences of our emotional acts and decisions. Through recklessness we can destroy our health and ourselves. We do not have endless energies; we have limits and boundaries. Life dictates that there exist limits. We can only do certain things up to certain points. What is more, the world remains full of emergency situations, and we cannot become the savior of the world. We cannot become messiahs. In other words, we do ourselves a great favor when we can say no to ourselves as well as to others. This very fact implies sitting down and reading and discerning what life says to us at a given significant moment. Otherwise some very painful consequences follow. We constantly need to take stock of particular experiences of our lives. We all need space around ourselves. When we respect boundaries and limits, we offer quality service in our lives.

The key lies with reflecting regularly on what goes on in our lives and on the consequences of our decisions and actions. Here it becomes important to recognize that we remain forever shaped by the forces within the immediate environment of our upbringing. As a result, we often reproduce traits of personalities who have been significant in our lives. When we give ourselves space and time to reflect on ourselves emotionally, we may, for example, become aware of how we might be building up anger slowly toward some particular people. And when we fail to become aware of our anger, we may simply throw it at people without reflecting on how it affects them. Lack of awareness of, for instance, the intensity of our anger can lead us to reckless acts. When we become aware of and own up to our intense feelings we can make resourceful decisions about them. Ultimately, we must, then, note that when we experience ourselves emotionally, we actually allow our inner reality to reveal itself to our immediate consciousness.

Notably, the communal origins of our existence foreground most of our relationships, together with our emotional needs and demands. Our interactive and interpretative origins affect us and our relationships in some very deep ways. Our community of origins actually gives deeper meaning to our relationship itself. Often our communal roots place us in contexts that inspire us, for example, with the conviction to emulate the examples of people who have achieved. Furthermore, our social starting points frequently teach us the value of reciprocity as necessary for healthy community and relational life; we learn how to try to reciprocate for all the goodness we experience in life. In effect, the hub of healthy relationships revolves around ongoing retrieval of our communal roots and values that cultivate harmony and our growth into fuller and resourceful persons— that is, sensitive and active listeners. When communal roots and ends inform our consciousness of relationships, they inform the processes of relating with one another emotionally. In other words, like a compass, healthy values and heritage of our communal life facilitate, enhance, and safeguard the ways and terms by which we emotionally negotiate the directions of our lives.

All the preceding considerations anticipate and point toward the character of a healthy relationship, some considerations to which the next section turns.

A HEALTHY RELATIONSHIP

A healthy relationship creates a supportive environment, which encourages us to grow and be ourselves. Within its sphere we let others be themselves and grow. This also means that we can be and grow together with others. That is to say, we grow to share values, interests, and goals. A certain accommodation, celebration, and exploration of the mystery of each person take place. The resulting relational climate then offers validation and understanding, as well as an emotional, physical, and intellectual sense of personal valuation. In other words, the acceptance that characterizes a healthy relationship frees persons to grow and become their authentic selves.

Clearly, as it enhances and does not absorb the self, a healthy relationship enables people to communicate needs, desires, and wishes clearly. Its characteristic emotional involvement and care further turn it into a cherished locus of strength that springs from the experience and expression of shared vulnerability. This is also to say, in its context people state their expectations clearly and allow others to fulfill their expectations as well. They accommodate and honor their insecurities along with the growth of trust. Then they open up their feelings to one another. They allow others access to their thoughts, ideas, and feelings. In short, they allow others into their lives.

Accordingly, a healthy relationship establishes itself on the experience of common ground or interests. In such a context, the partners or parties to a relationship not only feel attraction to one another but also like each other. They accept one another with freedom and honesty. This fact also means that they feel comfortable with one another as they share experiences, loyalty, and dependability. Within such a relational climate, trust and the sense of care and benevolence develop and grow.

At its best, a healthy relationship expresses itself in friendships in which we ideally do not hold back our dreams, successes, weaknesses, or failures. In short, when we find ourselves with our true friends, we feel comfortable. In the presence of true friends, we can be our best selves and readily express our goodness. Also, our true friends counsel, warn, and rebuke us; they alert us to risks and in so doing, keep us from mistakes we might make.

The nurturing and safe framework of a healthy relationship positively engages and motivates all it touches and embraces. It inspires life with confidence and a sense of responsibility. In a healthy relationship, people recognize and listen to their own truth of life and wherever it leads them. The setting of a wholesome relationship institutes listening as an important part of communication that allies itself with the desire and aspiration to disclose oneself in concrete experiences. The transparency, comfort, and enlivenment that mark a listening relationship provide much safeguard against distrust and pretense. As a form of dialogue, listening requires several elements: objectivity and accommodation, attention and patience, quality of presence, empathy and a gentle approach, respect for the other and self-transcendence, and a sense of commonness.

It must be pointed out here that empathy refers to accurately hearing, understanding, and communicating that understanding. It refers to the skill of communicating feelings—namely, accurately sensing the emotional world of another person. The summoning of the reflection of feelings coincides with empathy; its healing effects derive from the experience that "we are no longer alone" in a given context. We get to know that someone understands us. Through empathy we sense and understand another person from a unique and appropriate perspective. Empathy comes through listening that understands how people feel and live in the world (i.e., how they use their world).

Within the setting of a workable, viable, and healthy relationship listening truly becomes an art, a skill, and a discipline. Good listening enables us to reach one another at the level of feeling. Or again, mindfulness of the other characterizes all good listening. We show that we listen through our word, body posture, touch, voice, and action messages. In this regard, people who prefer "I" messages to "you" messages nurture and build up positive relations with one another. The preference of I to you messages allows for the distinction between the I and you as essential poles in every authentic relationship, where individuals assume responsibility for their own thoughts, feelings, and actions. Further, I messages tend to cause less defensiveness in the other while you messages easily lead to blame and judgmental attitudes. As we prefer I to you messages, we bring out and mold a genuine impression and a true picture of the other. Of course, we must also observe that I and you messages can always express themselves through actions, which may indicate anger, interests, fatigue, boredom, or flight, for example.

As people try to become rewarding listeners, they communicate affirmatively and show that they know, or grow to know, one another other as well as the self. In the process, rewarding listening builds trust and stability in relationships as it also acts as a bridge-maker. Where people listen well to each other, they manifest respect and acceptance toward the mosaic that each person comes to represent and symbolize. This also means ongoing self-respect and self-acceptance and respect and acceptance of others. People open up and become truly available to one another.

Of course, relational discipline remains essential to the health and success of every compassionate and understanding relationship. This discipline refers to the capacity for self-mastery and self-transcendence, which further signifies self-control, self-conquest, and self-denial. Relational discipline nurtures the growth of honest and humane behaviors. Self-discipline contrasts with self-gratification, pride, and compulsion, which depend on short-lived emotions and instincts. In fact, lack of discipline impairs a person's capacity for kind and generous judgments that promote and enliven wholesomeness among people.

Also, helpful responses mark healthy relationships. We respond helpfully in a relationship when we reflect feelings and reasons and avoid unrewarding "don'ts." It means refraining from judgmental attitudes and from taking control over what the other person says, judges, and does. Indeed, how a person responds to another can indicate security, attraction, tenderness, care, and support, or any other perspectives and feelings of security in life. It can also indicate distance, hurt, jealousy, and confusion. People who moralize, blame, and preach in relationships frequently fail to duly recognize, reward, and accept the other person as they reveal themselves in performance in the world. Besides, labeling, over-interpretation, irrelevance, or continual talking undercut good rapport among people. Certainly, having a proper sense of personal, intimate, public, and social zones honors and respects the significance of others.

The hold of a healthy relationship in people's lives confirms, consoles, and challenges them amidst all the joy, grief, gladness, and anxieties that form the staples of daily living. When people reach out and do not take each other for granted, they affirm and give one another due attention. In the process, they create a welcome space that attracts liveliness, offers care, and enables wellbeing.

What is more, in a healthy relationship people frequently learn to develop the art to self-activate themselves emotionally. In the process, they grow in assuming responsibility for the quality of their relationships with others. And as people experience and express their life situations realistically, they also enhance and enrich their lives with vitality, vigor, and an empowering sense of aliveness. In this way, they readily acknowledge opportunities that nourish and strengthen them with delight, gladness, pleasure, and joy. In addition, when people offer their energies, time, convenience, money, and resources to share life with others, they show that they value and cherish them. The resulting experience and felt sense of security in life make possible right, appropriate, and good ways of expressing feelings in truthful, gentle, and responsible ways. The emotional resources that we bring to a relationship shape the sense of who we are, the quality of our involvement with others, and who we desire to become.

Of course, a healthy relationship does not simply operate on naïve trust, mere romantic care, or sentimental forgiveness. Rather, it anchors itself in genuine enthusiasm, spiritual fervor, and true joy by means of which people also learn the art of self-giving. This art requires of people that they steadily free themselves from the stifling exigencies of paralyzing fear, urgings for survival and self-preservation, and overweening self-interests, greed, and power. The encouraging and comforting character of healthy relationships further embraces personal nurturance and self-protection. In this way, a relationship becomes a dwelling place of honor wherein people can make sacrifices for one another. This means that they rejoice and hope in one another so that they affirm and lift up each other. When people love and understand one another they reflect the inner beauty of human relationality.

Thus far, we now consider how appropriation of Christian intuitions nurtures the community of disciples as the family of God in which words and deeds relate closely and in life-giving ways.

CHRISTIAN INTUITIONS AND THE FAMILY OF GOD

To become efficacious agents and builders of the community of disciples as the family of God, Christians need to appropriate Christian intuitions at the levels of basic understanding, perceptions, and candor. This appropriation represents and accelerates conversion at levels that involve the crossing of critical conventional and ideological barriers. In one sense, conversion marks the dawn of a new realism and positive commitment to life so that a person genuinely deals with issues, challenges, and problems of existence. The internalization of Christian intuitions leaves its imprint on convictions, judgments, attitudes, and imaginations that stimulate fresh thinking and that mirror themselves in gracious behaviors and conduct. When the living out of basic Christian theological intuitions commences, it resets and informs a person's existence and involvement in this world. In this way, the appropriation of basic Christian intuitions shapes personal interests, thought, and acceptable practices that also re-create the constantly changing realities and circumstances of individual and shared life. In other words, the illumination that comes with Christian theological intuitions reorients guidance, inspiration, and imagination, which provide practical counsels for daily living.

To put it starkly, Christian intuitions coincide with the revelation of Jesus as the Son of God, the revelation of the God of Jesus as referring to the God he revealed, and the revelation of salvation that Jesus brings as coming from God that he disclosed.

The Christian life refers us to the revelation of Jesus Christ in the gospels. As paradigmatic and normative of full human life, Jesus makes manifest the fundamentals of Christian life. As God's gift of grace, Jesus exemplifies the Christian living out of the light of the mystery of God. To follow Jesus involves appropriating his message and imitating him. Jesus expresses fully God's generous, merciful, and self-giving love. At the same time, as the fullest expression of humanity, Jesus's patterns of life set up the basis of the good Christian life. In other words, authentic Christian life conforms to the guiding patterns and image of Jesus Christ as revealed in the gospels and kept alive by the community of disciples called the Church.

As the gospels reveal, in Jesus God becomes the ultimate object of loyalty. This God Jesus calls Father. Jesus's life and efficacious presence coincides with God involved in and with the world. In fact, the whole life of Jesus points firmly toward the primacy of love and understanding that do not alienate living truth. That God loves us lies at the heart of Christian living itself. In practice, then, Christians strive to creatively adapt Jesus's wisdom, sayings, actions, teachings, spirit, and basic attitudes toward life as a whole. The frames of Jesus's deeds, words, and attitudes enable us to recognize what carries significance, worth, and efficacy. They also shape the ideas and values that define the way we respond to new situations, new issues, and new questions.

In fact, Jesus proclaimed the reign and presence of God's love. This God, revealed as always with us, makes it possible to develop a holistic interpretation of God, humanity, and the historical world. God acts in and through historical events. Human history and consciousness of the deeds of God belong together. God freely engages the events of history with the deep exigencies of promise and fulfillment. In other words, within the contingency of events, God's creative action takes place, and this action gives human history some integrity, meaning, and direction. In one sense, God grounds the unity comprising the indwelling connections between the events in history. Human history does not exist outside God's transcendent freedom.

Jesus's open-hearted disposition with respect to mercy, forgiveness, unconditional availability, and abiding pointedness toward God celebrates the meaning of true humanity even in light of its multiplicity of concrete aspects. Subsequently, Christian life entails responsibility for our attitudes and behaviors amidst much ambivalence and risk that attend concrete judgments, choices, and actions.

In a word, Jesus came to create the family of God to which all belong. This family of service and inclusiveness recognizes and exalts in the affirming worth of all. As a dwelling place of blessings, liberation, and understanding, this family requires that people learn to trust and commit to the wellbeing of one another. It further implies building up relational bonds that celebrate the gift and significance of every people. Or again, positive relations among people foster love that enables people to become their best selves. As soon as people create and enjoy friendships, companionship, and life-giving relationships, they also nurture sensitivities, responsiveness, and a vision of true familyhood. Where people make room for one another, it means that they exalt in each other's being. When every member of God's family opens up, each becomes a credible symbol of inclusive love, liberative living, and expansive freedom. In the end, each

Christian disciple can make care, life-giving warmth, and communion basic staples of ordinary life.

In light of the preceding considerations, it becomes evident that for God things have value insofar as they sustain and expand our togetherness and lived experience of kinship. As a matter of life and death, this also implies equality of all as brothers and sisters of the same quality, without which peace and unity cannot be realized truly. Where inequality exists, the potential for conflicts and violence exists. In the end, the measure of sainthood and holiness becomes the experience and expression of our brotherhood and sisterhood—namely, our human fellowship with one another. Any other way risks becoming and remaining problematic. Sin, then, coincides with whatever undermines our experience and expression of togetherness as brothers and sisters of the same quality. Fellowship in the one God remains the criterion for distinguishing the human good from the bad. This criterion for judging enables us to know what needs to be done and for processing new forms of being Church.

Moreover, what we believe becomes spirit. Namely, it leads to spirituality as a central way or approach to life. And the spirituality of familyhood exalts the wisdom of constructive dialogue and the gift of our persons. The spirituality of familyhood includes the awareness that contention over signature issues need constructive engagement, dialogue, negotiations, and compromise. All these relational and interpretational approaches further demand that people respectfully reach out to one another. Of course, cooperation, competition, friendship, and tensions mark the family of God all the time. Yet the continual dynamics of patience, hard work, dialogue, and understanding resonate with a bright future of achievable human familyhood.

FIDELITY, PRAYER, AND THE CHURCH AS FAMILY

Fidelity to the spirit of Church as family entails familiarity with the most personal, most characteristic, and most important aspects of people's lives—that is, their interior lives. Surprisingly, however, people tend to ignore or neglect their interiority. Fidelity to the spirit of Church as family requires that believers remain open to the voice of the Spirit in the community life or living life with others. This fidelity cannot be separated from exploring the profound reality that God personifies communion and love, which culminate in a relationship of oneness of spirit. Belief in the power of the Spirit who cooperates with our liberty in existence essentially makes others brothers and sisters. Also, as it centers the self on God, the Spirit liberates people from interior disregard for the lives and concerns of others.

As the Spirit makes the God of Jesus present, the experience unifies our lives and relationships. Dichotomies become unified wholes. Where God becomes alive, he holds and brings all things and people together. This transforming experience particularly expresses itself in the ordinary routines of cooperative and pleasant life lived day by day. When the experience of the God of Jesus Christ imbues us, we feel a deeper liberty of spirit and joy. It also opens us up to a renewed horizon of sincerity, concern, and hope, which implicate a mysterious interplay between human disposition and divine intervention. Further, when we hope, we live with a spirit of basic trust and confidence in life so that active restlessness propels and enables us to make enriching impacts onto the world. In this way, we make possible and realizable the unfolding of the future kingdom of God in the present.

Tellingly, to grow in the availability characteristic of the family of God, we need to be people deeply rooted in prayer. Fidelity in prayer implies an active and continuous struggle against the forces of interior dissipation, as also against the blindness and trivialities that come with habits of shallowness. It remains the case that the God to whom we give our fidelity can be betrayed. In effect, fidelity requires continual renewal in order for it to remain creative.

Nonetheless, where fidelity in prayer expresses itself unmistakably, patience and humility gaze from the depths of its nature. Such fidelity recognizes God as someone permanent, continuing, and who implies salvational history. In this way, prayer links the human consciousness itself with the assurance of the living God, the absolute, the God of Jesus Christ. Prayer rooted in fidelity necessarily seems precarious, but it rests on a certain appeal delivered from the depths of our own insufficiency *ad summam altitudinem*, the absolute resort.[2] This appeal further presupposes a radical humility in the human subject. In the circumstances, it also becomes a matter of extending an infinite credit to God who becomes one's all.

2. Marcel, *Creative Fidelity*, 167.

Insofar as it roots itself in a person's life, prayer then renews, re-inforces, and refines the depth and breadth of interiority, attitudes, and personal presence. In this way, prayer gives shape to life's direction and a sense of purpose. In prayer, as we communicate with and surrender *who we are* to God, we emerge into a region where transcendence takes on the aspect of love expressible in forms such as, "never enough, always more, always closer." The illuminations and changes that follow always remain gradual, partial, and progressive. They also manifest themselves responsibly, finitely, imaginatively, and communally. In other words, a life of deep spirituality realizes itself over time and space, and it also requires discipline, sacrifice, and generosity.

When God remains the subject of our prayers, we also recognize ourselves as recipients of God's activities. Admittedly, we truthfully grant that we remain works in progress and need to leave room for God to continue shaping and molding us. We need change in our lives, which entails taking prayerful positions before God without having to competitively compare ourselves to others. When we are ourselves, we also become honest with God. As we grow in honesty and good faith we withhold unnecessary criticisms of others and more often than not give others the benefit of the doubt in our dealings with them. We also become willing to be surprised by others' growth in goodness and beauty. When we give others space and time to grow, we enable them to change and develop right relationships in their lives. In this sense, we expand the foothold of justice in common life.

As we tap into the inward resources of our interiority, we shape and change resourcefully the exterior of our lives. We affect our perceptions of and activities in the outside world. Tapping on the inside enables us to function and thrive on the outside. We constructively organize our life again.

CONCLUSION

This chapter offered insights and perspectives important for Christians and human relationships in a world continually ridden with relational difficulties. In our times, few people escape the pains that accompany relationships. Love of friend and respect for humanity do not always take place in relationships. People enter relationships with varying levels of receptivity of their own truth (i.e., with varying moral and spiritual sensitivities and capacities). Still, ideological, economic, social, and political crosswinds influence people's behaviors and attitudes toward their own relationships. This also means that as long as we remain human, we cannot shield ourselves from the fragility and weaknesses that characterize interpersonal relationships. Yet through wise choices and judgments within relationships, we can always impact people's lives and society as a whole positively.

Consequently, this chapter sought to articulate the kind of wisdom that would minimize, if not cast out, fear and stimulate goodwill in human relationships. Such wisdom not only illuminates the truly human, but it also creates a responsible sense of boundaries necessary for enhancing the quality of human relations. While it remains a precarious and vulnerable adventure, people always need to face, work through, and transfigure the realities of pain and things gone wrong in their lives and relationships without triggering further harm and conflict. When we face and resourcefully deal with unspoken expectations and whispers of fears that we bring into relationships, we grow in responsible behaviors. Also, we must be mindful of the fears, concerns, and interests of the other person with whom we relate. The thrust of such awareness enables us to fashion our relationships appropriately. In this way, our relationships begin to bear witness to faith, hope, love, truth, and justice. Otherwise, human relationships easily become repositories of brutalization, violence, and death.

As we seek to redress wrongs and make justice in our relationships, we can fall prey to our self-centered selves. In this respect, we must also face the issues of inner freedom and the sense of responsibility that protect us against an over-possessive enthusiasm about our relationships. Where inner freedom and responsibility prevail, we flourish as relational beings. Within this framework, it further becomes important to recognize that awakening to our own emotional vulnerability as human beings does help nurture our own sense of care and sensitivity in life as a whole. It also enables us to rejoice in one another as we participate in a common relational adventure.

When it comes to the issue of sexuality in relationships, we must immediately affirm that it involves the human needs, demands, and expressions for love, communion, community, friendship, self-perpetuation, family, humor, and self-transcendence. Furthermore, all these elements entail contact with and surrender to the personality, personal sensitivities, and respect for the other as a person toward whom responsibility must become manifested.

Of course, relationships always remain definite yet also porous. They continually challenge and invite us to become our better selves. The accepting and transforming power of engaging relationships draws people closer to one another through its sensibilities of hedging in and separateness, interdependence and communion. In this way, we find within the ambiguous character of every relationship its potential to liberate or the risk to stifle our changing definitions of what it means to be alive meaningfully.

In fact, rarely does relational life present itself as straightforward and calm for most people. More often than not, people in relationships meet all kinds of hazards that upset or disclose their apparent emotional balance or insecurity. When we participate in relational and emotional drama, the experience readily surprises or disorganizes us by its sheer unfamiliarity until we achieve some adequate and functional adaptation. Thus, the ambiguity, dangers, and temptations that mark human relationships also bring with them broad and intense opportunities for awakening that highlight, clarify, and rearrange our human self-perceptions and self-definitions. Our experience of every relational wilderness (as we become negative, hypercritical, and disloyal emotionally) brings with it a lot of potential and opportunities, even amidst its dangers. In other words, the freeing and creative experience of renewal always accompanies the changes and challenges that we embrace.

In this context, recollection always enables people to get in touch with their own sense of intrinsic worth. That is to say, it behooves people not to ground their sense of personal worth on the belief in the apparent nonworth of others. Or again, the experience of inwardness stirs people into simultaneously recognizing their own humanity as well as that of others. It also enables people to come to terms with their own unresolved personal issues and expectations so that they cultivate a truer image of themselves within relationships.

In accordance with this perspective, we may note that when we find ourselves in a situation of growth, we start to train ourselves in the habits of reflection, understanding, and discernment. In the process, we develop our perceptions and practices of humanity, of service, and of solidarity with one another. In all cases, it becomes a matter of pursuing, echoing, and heralding new forms of relationships which spring from new awareness and deep tones of felt human kinship. In this awareness, we further temper our own enthusiasm with an understanding of the predicament of others to whom we then communicate support, respect, and friendship.

When the wisdom of positive and liberative relationships becomes the living reality in the hearts of many priests, religious people, laity, politicians, and civil servants, people truly enhance the spirit of human familyhood. When the liberty of positive energy pervades human relationships, people experience and radiate peace, joy, and love. They become authentic as they strive to live life in new ways. Within this context and as Christians we then communicate our faith through the witness and example that we give by our actions in the service of the human family. We also contribute to ongoing social reconstruction when we inspire life with enthusiasm, involvement, and the deep sense of attachment to hope and the joy of living.

Conclusion

THE METAPHOR OF THE Church as family manifests critical reflection on the work of faith and culture in the light of the gospel, and the model of the Church as family arises from the commitment of the Christian community to the struggle for liberation from captive forms of existence. Furthermore, the Church as family roots itself in the profound perception of Christian hope and liberty and the spirit of fundamental human kinship. The internal workings of this model encourage and expand human availability. It also endows human interactions with the liveliness of mutual self-gift and the fullness of presence. The foregoing affirmations remain important because our often pompous, self-centered, and arrogant world can easily inflame the passion of individuals of goodwill with an exaggerated sense of self-importance and the exigencies of industrial capitalism.[1]

In fact, as a horizon from which Christians illuminate their lives, the Church as family makes up a milieu in which Christians rejoice and exult in the beautiful experiences, joyful moments, and enlivening encounters that life offers. When the Church as family embodies critical reflection on praxis in the light of faith, it guides daily realities that form the sense of who people are, directs the mainspring of understanding and wisdom, and steers people's love for the common good of the human community. When the Church as family becomes the symbol of Christian praxis, it fosters the sense and practice of civic responsibility and generates increasingly assertive actions that serve the needs of people disfigured and bent by social oppression and control. This entails both striving to eliminate poverty and unhealthy discrimination in the world and adopting the world sense *of the struggle for liberation*.

---

1. The exigencies of industrial capitalism include maximum profit at lowest costs, valuation of speed, primacy of analytical and technological thinking over reconstructive symbolic thinking of human relations, atomization of human beings, and the tendency to regard people as units of production who can deliver certain output.

Accordingly, a part of the task of the Church as family consists in embodying and safeguarding the transcendence of the human person and living ties among people through justice and love, within the sociocultural and historical contexts of existence. Essentially, the Church as family strives to generate opportunities for positive dialogue that create an order wherein people can become free or at least orient themselves toward becoming free for transcendence in communion. Through her activities inspired by the Spirit of Jesus and the gospel, the Church as family then aims to surmount and transform repressive attitudes and structures. In the Church as family it becomes evident that people mature and become genuinely human when they open themselves up to others through the sacrifice and offering of themselves in order to serve others. Of course, it must be noted that only in freedom can people truly direct themselves toward human goodness, which creates value and enduring meaning.

In addition, we do well when we understand the Church as family in terms of Christian discipleship as the following of Jesus Christ. This fact also means that in the family of God, people communicate with one another. They also challenge the attitudes and tendencies that encumber and disable them from reaching out to others with kindness and compassion. In a profound commitment to a common humanity of people and the unconditional lovableness of human individuals, the Church as family opposes, disputes, and argues with any work of violence and violation of people.

Within the foregoing framework, inculturated faith validates local actions that derive their inspirations from the person of Jesus Christ and his message. Such actions also usually provide room for practical critical intentions as well as the countenance of being in life. Indeed, within the life of faith we cannot replace mysticism and spirituality with the socially manifested expressions of Christian discipleship. The radical dimension of interiority involves liturgical recollectedness and worship as well as personal prayer. The interior life lies at the root of all human repentance and conversion. After all, outward comfort and calm can easily conceal inward enslavement to selfishness, vice, greed, and violence of the heart. The dialectics between earthly liberation and eschatological hope cannot be separated in the heart of being the Church. This dialectics sets limits on our judgments, actions, and activities. Here we may note that unrestrained thoughts, imaginations, and desires easily lead to uncontrolled actions, conflicts, and confusions with horrendous and abhorrent ecclesial consequences.

In reflecting on the Church as family, the following counsels must also be granted. First, there exist multiple ways of being Church. Circumstance, time, and place inspire and influence the particular embodiment and expressions of being Church. Second, multiple understandings and expressions mediate different ways of life and Christian discipleship. In effect, the Church as family does not exhaust the totality of Christian discipleship and Christian witness. In other words, the validity of the Church as family depends on its adequacy to particular experiences and fidelity to the Christian tradition. The Church as family represents and captures one important and efficacious pursuit of Christian freedom and the truth of human fullness. It veritably concretizes itself with regard to particular experiences.

Yet, as the necessity of integrating faith and culture correctly recognizes, the Church as family bases itself on a universality that roots itself in the concrete experience of people. In our contemporary world, where true regard for the "other" appears to diminish in certain respects, civility and common decency in human relations also become spurious as winning ways define the importance of successful living. In contrast with these stifling approaches toward life, the Church as family must provide alternative predispositions and visions. As a placeholder of human exaltation and familiarity, the Church as family spreads the sense of responsibility and warm-heartedness consistent with fruitful and sweet exchanges among people of different cultures. In other words, in an increasingly secular world, we need room for spiritual sensibility in our lives and relationships. This also implies a certain turning away from overweening self-preoccupation so that we can orient ourselves in meaningful ways to God, others, and the world around us.

With great earnestness, rich thought, and vivid narrative, life in the Church as family, as a countervailing and transforming metaphor, becomes worthwhile. Such life can beautify a person with startling and breathtaking vitality and dynamics of wellbeing. Conversely, when we reduce the itinerary of life to matters of eternal principles and claims to power, the logic and calculus of human expendability and demolition govern relationships as we also display open disregard for diversity. We then do much harm to common or shared life. Only when we live without fear or unwarranted fervor can we heal relationships and deal with tensions of life satisfactorily, amicably, and significantly. Unity of purpose and the desire and discipline to stand by wholesome truth improve human accountability. They also endow life with honest interactions that, in effect, move humanity forward as people create communities of honor and fairness in their dealings with one another.

In the end, it cannot be denied that the wisdom of Christ in the Church as family privileges and prompts us with creative spirit and the sense of imagination. And the privileging of the creative spirit and imagination helps us to face relational challenges and the diversity of our societies in fresh and fulfilling ways. It also makes it possible for us to develop a critical sense as we interpret and understand the world around us in ways that open up new horizons and deepen our perspectives on living out the values of Jesus Christ. For this reason, through the creative spirit and imagination that Christian faith inspires we build up ourselves and our various communities. All this particularly takes place as we begin to put to responsible and best use our gifts, talents, and capacities that uplift our own sense of esteem and felt dignity.

Bibliography

Abbott, Walter M., ed. *The Documents of Vatican II: All Sixteen Official Texts Promulgated by the Ecumenical Council.* New York: Guild, 1966.

Ackroyd, Peter R. "The Book of Isaiah." In *The Interpreter's One-Volume Commentary of the Bible: Introduction and Commentary for Each Book of the Bible Including Apocrypha*, Charles M. Laymon, ed. Nashville, Tennessee: Abingdon (1990) 329–71.

Africa Faith and Justice Network. *African Synod: Documents, Reflections, Perspectives.* Maryknoll, New York: Orbis, 1996.

Baur, John. *The Catholic Church in Kenya: A Centenary History.* Nairobi, Kenya: Paulines Publications Africa, 1990.

Burns, J. Patout. *Cyprian the Bishop.* London: Routledge, 2002.

Berquist, John L., ed. *Strike Terror No More: Theology, Ethics, and the New War.* St Louis, Missouri: Chalice, 2002.

Brown, Raymond E. *The Churches the Apostles Left Behind.* New York: Paulist, 1984.

Clifford, Richard J. "Isaiah 40–66." In *Harper's Bible Commentary*, James L. Mays, ed. San Francisco: HarperSanFrancisco (1988) 571–96.

Coggins, Richard J. "Do We Still Need Deutero-Isaiah?" *Journal for the Study of the Old Testament* 81 (1998) 77–92.

Dulles, Avery. *The Assurance of Things Hoped For.* New York: Oxford University Press, 1994.

———. *Models of the Church.* New York: Image, 2002.

Fraile, Peter A. *God Within Us: Movements, Powers and Joys.* Chicago: Loyola University Press, 1986.

Gallagher, Michael Paul. *Clashing Symbols: An Introduction to Faith and Culture.* New York: Paulist, 1998.

Geerz, Clifford. *The Interpretation of Cultures.* New York: Basic, 1973.

Gelpi, Donald L. *Committed Worship: A Sacramental Theology for Converting Christians Vol. 1: Adult Conversion and Initiation.* Collegeville, Minnesota: Liturgical, 1993.

———. *Committed Worship: A Sacramental Theology for Converting Christians Vol. 2: The Sacraments of Ongoing Conversion.* Collegeville, Minnesota: Liturgical Press, 1993.

———. *As We Are One: A Study of Church Doctrine.* Unpublished Manuscript, 2005.

Goulder, Michael. "Deutero-Isaiah." *Journal for the Study of the Old Testament* 28 (2004) 351–62.

Haight, Roger. *Dynamics of Theology.* New York: Paulist, 1990.

Hughes, Robert. *Culture of Complaint: The Fraying of America.* New York: Oxford University Press, 1993.

Marcel, Gabriel. *Problematic Man.* New York: Herder & Herder, 1967.

———. *Creative Fidelity.* New York: Crossroad, 1982.

Bibliography

McGary, Cecil. "The Church as Family: Sign and Instrument of the Unity of the Whole Human Race." In *New Strategies for a New Evangelization in Africa*. Patrick Ryan, ed. Nairobi, Kenya: Paulines Publications Africa (2002) 28–43.

McKenzie, John L. *The Anchor Bible: Second Isaiah*. Garden City, New York: Doubleday, 1968.

Niebur, H. Richard. *Christ and Culture*. New York: Harper & Row, 1951.

Pelletier, Anne-Marie. "Isaiah." In *The International Bible Commentary: A Catholic and Ecumenical Commentary for the Twenty-First Century*, William R. Farmer, ed. Collegeville, Minnesota: Liturgical (1998) 957–97.

Ruwaichi, Jude Thaddaeus. "Inculturating the Gospel and Evangelizing Culture." In *New Strategies for a New Evangelization in Africa*. Patrick Ryan, ed. Nairobi, Kenya: Paulines Publications Africa (2002) 47–53.

———. "The Newness and Pastoral Implications of the Church as a Family." In *New Strategies for a New Evangelization in Africa*. Patrick Ryan, ed. Nairobi, Kenya: Paulines Publications Africa (2002) 23–27.

Schneiders, Sandra. *Revelatory Text: Interpreting the New Testament as Sacred Scripture*. Collegeville, Minnesota: Liturgical, 1999.

Schreiter, Robert J. *Constructing Local Theologies*. Maryknoll, New York: Orbis, 1986.

Sobrino, Jon. *Where is God? Earthquake, Terrorism, Barbarity, and Hope*. Maryknoll, New York: Orbis, 2004.

Stuhmueller, Carroll, "Deutero-Isaiah." In *The Jerome Biblical Commentary*, Raymond E. Brown, ed. Englewood Cliffs, New Jersey: Prentice-Hall (1968) 366–86.

Sullivan, Francis A. *From Apostles to Bishops: The Development of Episcopacy in the Early Church*. New York: Newman, 2001.

Tanner, Kathryn. *Theories of Culture: A New Agenda for Theology*. Minneapolis: Fortress, 1997.

Tidwell, Neville. "The Cultic Background of Isaiah 40:1–11." *Journal of Theology for Southern Africa* 3 (1973) 41–54

Tillich, Paul. *Dynamics of Faith*. New York: Harper & Brothers, 1956.

Watts, John D. W. *Word Biblical Commentary*, Vol. 25: Isaiah 34–66. Waco, Texas: Word, 1987.